THE MOSELLE
River and Canal from the Roman Empire
to the European Economic Community

University of Toronto
DEPARTMENT OF GEOGRAPHY
RESEARCH PUBLICATIONS

The Moselle River and Canal from the Roman Empire to the European Economic Community

Jean Cermakian

PUBLISHED FOR THE UNIVERSITY OF TORONTO
DEPARTMENT OF GEOGRAPHY
BY THE UNIVERSITY OF TORONTO PRESS
TORONTO AND BUFFALO

© University of Toronto Department of Geography 1975
Published by University of Toronto Press
Toronto and Buffalo
Printed in Canada

Library of Congress Cataloging in Publication Data

Cermakian, Jean, 1940-
The Moselle: river and canal from the Roman Empire to the European
Economic Community.

(Research publications – University of Toronto Department of Geography; 14)
Revised version of the author's thesis, University of California, 1967.
Bibliography: p.
1. Moselle River – Navigation – History. 2. Moselle River – Regulation –
History. 3. Stream channelization – Moselle River – History. I. Title.
II. Series: Toronto. University. Dept. of Geography. Research publications; 14
TC656.M6C47 1975   386'.3'094343   75-22132
ISBN 0-8020-3310-5

To the memory of my father,
Balthazar Cermakian
who taught me so much

Preface

This study owes its origin to my interest in the economic, political, and geographic aspects of what is generally called "European integration," i.e., the attempt (in some ways very successful, in others not) by nine European states to establish an economic community which could eventually lead to a political federation. It is because integration can only come about after standardizing transport networks and establishing a common transport policy that I have undertaken to study a waterway which to many symbolizes the "European spirit." Only with such great achievements as the canalization of the Moselle River can the building of a united Europe become a reality. This study goes back to the historical sources of the project with all its wars, quarrels, rivalries, and feuds which indicate that it is rather risky to be over-optimistic concerning easy solutions. The road to European unity is a long and difficult one, as the story of the Moselle project will show.

I am very grateful to the French government's Centre National de la Recherche Scientifique for its financial support in the form of a research fellowship for the academic year 1964-65, which allowed me not only to study the problems of European integration at the College of Europe in Bruges, Belgium, for several months, but also to carry out research and field work for this study, not only along the Moselle valley, but also in Brussels, Luxembourg, and Paris. During my stay in Europe, I was fortunate enough to receive the assistance of a great number of individuals and organizations. They are too numerous to be mentioned here, but all of them deserve my most sincere gratitude. I owe a special debt to the following: Dr I.B.F. Kormoss, Professor at the College of Europe, Bruges, Belgium; Mr Robert Planchar of the Direction des Transports of the European Economic Community Commission headquarters in Brussels; Mr Léon Hild, Director of Public Relations of the Société Internationale de la Moselle (G.m.b.H.) in Trier, West Germany; Mr Ivan Debois, Head of the Direction des Transports of the European Coal and Steel Community High Authority headquarters in Luxembourg, and Mr Reum of the European Communities Statistical Office, also in Luxembourg; Mr Mange, Secretary-General of the European Conference of Ministers of Transport in Paris; the Head of the Statistical Division of the Office National de la Navigation in Paris; Mr M. Lecavelier, Chairman of CAPEM (Comité d'Aménagement du Plan d'Equipement de la Moselle) in Metz, and his assistant, Mme de Saint-Maurice; Mr Henri Luja, Head of the Direction de l'Urbanisme, Mr Léon Geisen of the Ministère des Transports, Mr Méris, Secretary of the Chambre des Députés, and Mr Pierre Hamer, Director of the Société du Port Fluvial de Mertert S.A., all four in Luxembourg.

This study is a considerably revised version of my dissertation for the degree of Doctor of Philosophy in geography submitted and approved at the University of California (Berkeley) in August 1967. I would like to express my great appreciation for the suggestions and advice given by the members of the dissertation committee, Professors James E. Vance, Jr. (Chairman), Clarence J. Glacken, and W. Norman Kennedy, by the other faculty members of the Geography Department at Berkeley, by Professor Jean Gottmann during his term as Visiting Professor at Berkeley in the Spring Semester of 1966, and by my fellow faculty members at the Département de géographie of Université Laval in Québec from 1967 to 1970, and to my colleagues of the Département des Sciences humaines of Université du Québec à Trois-Rivières since 1970. I would like to address a special note of thanks to my former colleague, Dr Jean Raveneau, then head of the Laboratoire de Cartographie of Université Laval and to his staff, as well as to my student assistant at Trois-Rivières, Miss Lucie Bournival for redrawing with so much care some of the original maps and graphs from the dissertation. Finally, I would like to express my sincere appreciation to Mrs Lydia Burton and Mrs Helga MacKinnon, under whose thorough editorial guidance it was possible to iron out some of the imperfections in this study and to include a German translation of my French *résumé*, to Mr R.I.K. Davidson, of the University of Toronto Press, and to the Social Sciences Research Council of Canada, whose generous grant made the publication possible within this *Research Publications* series.

JEAN CERMAKIAN
Directeur, Module de géographie
Université du Québec à Trois-Rivières
Trois-Rivières, Québec, Canada
September 1974

Contents

ix

Plates

Figures

Tables

Abbreviations

CECA   Communauté Européenne du Charbon et de l'Acier
CEE   Communauté Economique Européenne
CEMT   Conférence Européenne des Ministres de Transports
CFL   Société Nationale des Chemins de Fer Luxembourgeois
ECMT   European Conference of Ministers of Transport
ECSC   European Coal and Steel Community
EEC   European Economic Community
OSCE   Office Statistique des Communautés Européennes
ONN   France. Ministère de l'Equipement, Office National de la Navigation
RNIR   *Revue de la Navigation Intérieure et Rhénane*
SIM   Société Internationale de la Moselle (G.m.b.H.)
SNCB   Société Nationale des Chemins de Fer Belges
SNCF   Société Nationale des Chemins de Fer Français

Throughout this study, measurements are given in the metric system only, with the following abbreviations:

km	kilometer	t	metric ton
m	meter	ton-km	metric ton-kilometer

Foreign currencies are abbreviated as follows:

BF	Belgian Franc	DM	Deutsche Mark
FF	French Franc	RM	Reichs Mark
LF	Luxembourg Franc		

xiv

THE MOSELLE
River and Canal from the Roman Empire
to the European Economic Community

I

Introduction

THE THREEFOLD FUNCTION OF INLAND WATERWAYS

Transportation routes, from the very primitive to the greatly advanced, are among the most universal features in cultural (or man-made) landscapes. Even in highly primitive societies, transportation routes fulfill the basic economic need of movement through the forest to secure means of subsistence. At the other end of the economic development scale, modern transport structures are built with the idea of attaining (or maintaining) the highest possible living standards by fostering increasing interchange among as many different kinds of products as possible, and in large enough volume to make the per-unit cost of transport as low as possible.

The latter consideration leads to the examination of the three basic assumptions underlying the geography and economics of deep-draft water transportation:
1 "The waterway ... is especially well-suited to the transport of bulky, low per-unit value goods. It is therefore found in the initial and final stages of the development process."[1] In the initial stage, it is mostly used for the shipment of mineral raw materials and the receipt of basic economic products (e.g., coal, cement, etc.). In the final stage, it plays an important role in the transport competition for certain kinds of special products (e.g., steel tubes).
2 Inland water transport, given its primary function as a bulk carrier, helps to reinforce interregional links and complementarity between mining and industrial areas, such as coal basins and steel-producing districts. Furthermore, such links

1 Jean Labasse, *L'organisation de l'espace: éléments de géographie volontaire* (Paris: Hermann, 1966), p. 127. (Author's transl.)

3

might even be initiated by the waterway and thus benefit a hitherto isolated region (although the idea of "isolation" must always be a relative one). In this context, some French geographers and economists have coined the concept of désenclavement, which they define as "those coherent attempts undertaken by the governmental authorities to break the material and moral isolation of areas which would otherwise be condemned to economic stagnation or political secession."[2]

Such areas are thought of as enclaves or islands of actual or potential economic and social backwardness surrounded by more prosperous and progressive regions. 3 It has often been assumed by economic and planning experts and technicians that a deep-draft inland waterway is bound to create new industries and foster regional development by its very existence. A well-known example is the TVA system, although in that case it is difficult to evaluate the respective shares of increased river traffic and cheaper hydro-electric power in regional development; one would assume that the power factor was the more significant. Sharply in contrast were the role of the Erie Canal in opening up the Mohawk valley for agricultural settlement in the 1820s and the contribution of the Saint Lawrence Seaway in the establishment of many manufacturing plants along its Montréal-Lake Ontario section. These stand as examples of the catalytic role of inland navigation in regional development. .

So far, these three assumptions (or hypotheses) concerning inland navigation have been discussed in the most general terms. The remainder of this introduction shows how they apply to the European waterways system, of which the Moselle River is such an important segment.

The first and most important assumption – *the waterway as the prime carrier of bulky products* – is well justified by statistics of European inland water transport. According to an intergovernmental experts' report, "iron and steel, solid fuels, mineral oils, building materials, grain, and fertilizers play a predominant part in the overall traffic handled on western European waterways."[3]

The same report illustrates this statement by listing the percentages (by volume) of the six major groups of commodities transported on the Rhine at the Dutch-German border in 1964: iron ore (24 per cent), sand and gravel (12 per cent), crude oil and petroleum products (12 per cent), coal (9 per cent), chemical fertilizers (6 per cent), and grain (4 per cent).

The statistics for international goods transport published by the United Nations show that in 1971, West Germany imported about 82 million metric tons of goods by inland waterways (over one-quarter of the national import

2 Jean Labasse, *L'organisation de l'espace: éléments de géographie volontaire* (Paris: Hermann, 1966), p. 119. (Author's transl.)
3 CEMT, *Conseil des Ministres: Révolutions* **XVI**, 1966 (Paris: CEMT, 1967), 117 ("Rapport sur le rôle des voies navigables et sur leurs perspectives d'avenir").

total). Approximately 45 per cent of these imports were iron ore and petroleum products.[4]

In 1972 three-quarters of the total tonnage carried on French inland waterways consisted of raw or semi-processed minerals, construction materials, and petroleum products. If only internal traffic were considered, these categories made up almost 90 per cent of the total tonnage, solid mineral fuels and agricultural products being important mostly in foreign trade.[5]

Finally, in considering the inland waterways traffic in coal and steel products within the European Economic Community in recent years, one notices that three-quarters of the total movement is made up of coal and iron ore, whereas pig-iron, crude steel, and steel products account for about 15 per cent.[6]

The second assumption, *that the waterway serves as an interregional link,* is illustrated by many European examples. The Moselle River unites the Ruhr and Lorraine industrial areas. The Sambre and Meuse rivers in Belgium unite the coal-mining basin of the Borinage with the steel-producing Liège metropolitan area. In an example of désenclavement, the Albert Canal has made possible the industrialization of Belgian Limburg, and the Ghent-Terneuzen ship canal was built in part to allow the establishment of a large steel mill at Zelzate, on the Dutch-Belgian border.

The idea of interregional complementarity does not necessarily mean the linking of two industrial or mining regions. One of these may well be a large port area with many industries of its own, but having as its main function the transshipment to and from the major industrial center at the other end of the waterway. Examples of such links include the Rhône between Marseilles (Port-Saint-Louis-du-Rhône) and Lyons, the Seine between Le Havre and Paris, the Rupel between Antwerp and Brussels, and the Rhine between Rotterdam and Duisburg. Sometimes, such links are deliberately established at great expense and for political reasons, as in the case of the Albert Canal – an all-Belgian route between Liège and Antwerp built some 40 years ago parallel to the Dutch-Belgian border and still very heavily used.

Finally, the assumption *that a deep-draft waterway is of necessity a catalyst for regional development* may be debated on several grounds. First of all, the case of the Moselle will show that the new waterway, far from attracting new industry to the less-developed areas along its course (Eifel, Hunsrück), has instead reinforced the competitive position of the already heavily industrialized

---

4 United Nations, Economic Commission for Europe, *Annual Bulletin of Transport Statistics for Europe* (English/French/Russian), 23 (1971): 128, Table 30.

5 France, Ministère des Transports et Ministère de l'Equipement, Office National de la Navigation, *Statistique annuelle de la navigation intérieure: 1972* (Paris: ONN, 1973), 32-3.

6 OSCE, *Transports des produits du traité de la CECA: Année 1964, Série Transports,* No. 2, 1966 (Brussels-Luxembourg: OSCE, 1966), Table 14, p. 37.

5

regions at both ends, although this might change in the long run. Of course, this does not hold true for all new waterways, as is apparent in the case of the Albert Canal.

Secondly, the inertia of long-established industries in certain areas works against a decentralization of manufacturing. Therefore, the construction or improvement of a deep-draft waterway may have very little effect on the regional development of those areas which would benefit most from such decentralization. A striking example is the town of Huy on the Meuse, between Liège and Namur. The improvement of the riverbed and the building of new locks has not led to any visible new activities there, the inertia of the Liège industries being too great.

Thirdly, a new waterway by itself is not enough to foster economic development in a region. The national, regional, and local governments must be receptive to the idea of planning (with its consequent incentives and benefits) in order to attract new industries. Such was the case when the city of Chalon-sur-Saône created and equipped a large industrial park on the riverbank with good accessibility to rail and road transport. Local governments and private enterprise often have the enthusiasm but lack the funds. National governments, even though they are willing, must often choose not to develop a region as thoroughly as would be desirable, for political as well as financial reasons.

INLAND WATERWAYS AND EUROPEAN COOPERATION

From all that has been said so far, it is quite clear that the functions of a deep-draft waterways system are primarily economic. Such functions require a fairly flexible institutional framework so that goods might be carried by water with as few obstacles as possible. Until the end of the eighteenth century, the greatest of these obstacles was the incredible number of tolls levied by the many princes who controlled segments of all major European rivers. Thus inland navigation was hindered by the extreme political fragmentation which the European continent had inherited from the breakup of the Roman and Carolingian empires.

The French Revolution and Empire consolidated most of western and central Europe under a single authority between 1792 and 1814. It was thus very easy and convenient for the government of the French Republic to proclaim freedom of navigation on all European waterways.

At the Congress of Vienna (1815), the monarchs of Europe decided to codify the idea of free navigation and established the Central Rhine Commission the following year. The Commission is today the oldest existing international organization and has been continuously in operation since its founding. Its work of intergovernmental cooperation was reinforced by several conventions and agreements concerning navigation on the Rhine, its major tributaries (Main, Moselle, Neckar), the Meuse, and the Scheldt, between 1831 and 1956.[7]

These agreements, useful as they were for the expansion of commerce and industry during the Industrial Revolution, did not imply any surrender of national sovereignty by any of the States concerned. The idea of the omnipotent Nation-State was the basis of international relations during the nineteenth century and the first half of the twentieth. It was not challenged until the early 1950s. At that time, in spite of (and to a certain extent because of) the East-West political cleavage, some far-seeing Europeans such as Robert Schuman and Konrad Adenauer decided to try to unify western Europe's economic base. Economic integration would in turn, they hoped, lead to an eventual political federation. Their efforts led to the creation of the six-nation European Coal and Steel Community (ECSC) in 1951, which grew into the European Economic Community (EEC) in 1957. These two supranational organizations, along with the European Atomic Energy Community (EURATOM), also founded in 1957, began to merge into a single European Community with the merger of their respective executive branches into a single commission on 6 July 1967. In January 1973, three new members (Denmark, Eire, and the United Kingdom) joined the Community. In this new economic and political context, the old-fashioned waterways conventions and agreements are still useful but have become inadequate.

The European Conference of Ministers of Transport (ECMT), founded in Brussels in 1953, tried to fill the gap. It matched political cooperation and economic integration with an ambitious plan for the technical standardization of transport structures and equipment. This plan included three steps, as far as inland waterways were concerned:

1 The drafting of a 1953 resolution (amended in 1964) establishing a top-priority list of "waterways of interest to Europe as a whole" (voies d'eau d'intérêt européen). (See Table 1.)[8]

2 The decision to define standard dimensions for such waterways, existing or to be created (see Table 2), the 1350-ton class being referred to as the "European draft" (gabarit européen).

3 The definition of the standard dimensions of craft using this network (see Table 3).

In connection with the latter point, two technological advances have undoubtedly contributed to the standardization of European deep-draft waterways:

---

7 The integral texts of these conventions and agreements have been reproduced, with annotations, in C. Bonét-Maury (ed.), *Les Actes du Rhin et de la Moselle* (3rd ed.; Strasbourg: Les Editions de la Navigation du Rhin, 1966).

8 All tables in this study have been collected in the Statistical Appendix.

a the inclined plane, which has solved the problem of bottlenecks created by too many locks over too short a distance (witness the Ronquières inclined plane on the Brussels-Charleroi Canal, which has replaced 28 small locks).[9]

b the technique of navigation by pushing, i.e., the practice of pushing two 1600-ton barges with a small but powerful self-propelled craft, a technique which started in the United States on the Mississippi and Ohio rivers, and which is now very widely used on western European waterways such as the Rhine and the Moselle, being apparently preferred to the traditional navigation by towing or self-propelled craft.[10]

Technological advances, along with the successful evolution of western European economic integration, have made possible the beginnings of a common transportation network. But much remains to be done, for the European Community has failed so far to achieve a common transport policy, and without the latter no true economic integration is possible (see Figure 1).

POINTS OF VIEW

The problems raised by the creation or improvement of any transportation route must be approached in a certain perspective. The economist's concern in this respect is primarily one of estimating construction and transport costs, freight rates, tolls, and volumes of traffic in order to find out whether or not the proposed route would be economically viable, i.e., whether or not its construction would supplement or merely compete with existing routes and means of transport. His awareness of important historical, geographic, and political factors is subordinated to his immediate search for practical solutions upon which such factors should (but in his opinion do not always) have a far-reaching influence.

On the other hand, the historian's point of view is to explain the existing situation by referring to old documents, archives, and travel accounts. He is not concerned with projections or statistical analysis but believes that past events and situations should be the focus of his study because they are the only means by which the present can be explained — unlike the economist who starts with the present.

The political scientist tends to seek the solution in an analysis of national and regional decision-making processes and in an evaluation of individual and collective attitudes towards a given project. He may do so either in an historical perspective or only for the present situation.

The engineer is primarily interested in the technical aspects of the project at various stages of the nation's technological development. Here again, an historical approach would appear useful.

9 Pierre de Latil, "Entre Charleroi et Bruxelles, 28 écluses seront supprimées pour les péniches grâce au 'plan incliné' de Ronquières," *Le Figaro* (Paris), 1 September 1966.
10 "Le poussage sur le Rhin et la Moselle," *RNIR* 35 (1963): 626-3.

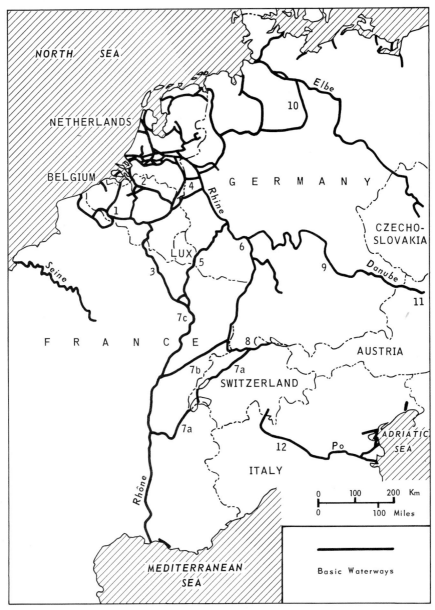

Figure 1 The CEMT waterways network. Established in 1953, this network project represents the first attempt to standardize European transport networks. The CEMT also recommended standardization of railroad and highway networks to its 18 member governments. The numbers on this map refer to the waterways listed in the Statistical Appendix, Table 1.

Finally, the geographer is interested in the route as a vector of human activity, especially with reference to changes brought by its construction to the areas it crosses, and to modifications in the patterns of interregional exchange after the completion of the project.

This is admittedly an oversimplified statement of different ways of approaching the same problem. But it makes the point that no single approach can satisfactorily solve the problem, and that for this reason there is a need for a composite approach which will vary according to the nature of the problem and the degree of complexity of its component parts.

In this study an effort is made to give proper weight to all possible approaches – economic, historical, political, technical, and geographic. But due to the nature of the available evidence, it has been necessary to stress the historical, political, and geographic approaches. Many valuable economic and technical writings on the Moselle have dealt with improvement and canalization projects; these are referred to often in the course of this study, not to paraphrase them, but to use them where they could help strengthen the argument as seen from the other three viewpoints. The nature of this problem particularly warrants a historical-political-geographic investigation.

Historical: Improvement or canalization of the Moselle has been planned and carried out with varying degrees of success for over nineteen centuries. Due to the strategic, political, and commercial importance of the Moselle valley since the Roman period, this route having always been one of the three natural corridors of trade between northern and southern Europe, the Moselle story has to be discussed against the background of major historical periods and events, such as the reign of Charlemagne, the wars of Louis xiv and Napoleon i, the French Revolution, the Franco-Prussian war, the two world wars, and the post-1945 drive towards European economic and political integration. Each of these has made a contribution – positive or negative – towards the solution of the problem.

Political: Perhaps the most important single conclusion about the Moselle problem is that economic and technological difficulties were never insuperable, but that for political reasons the river was never as fully utilized as it could have been. It was because of a politically favorable climate that the present project was finally implemented: the creation of the ECSC indirectly led to the solution of the Saar problem, which in turn led to the signature of the Moselle canalization convention. The evolution of political attitudes towards the project stress the magnitude of the real obstacles to its implementation.

Geographic: The actual and possible influence of the river's improvement and canalization projects (over 19 centuries) on the regional economies of Lorraine and the Palatinate, as well as the role of the Moselle as a catalyst for expanded North-South trade and interregional exchange is necessarily an important factor in the discussion of this waterway development.

10

Even with such an emphasis, this study is admittedly superficial. It is not meant as a methodological contribution to transportation geography, for there is no single best approach to the research problems in this field. Emphasis should vary with every given situation, as has been stressed before in this introduction.[11] Broad generalizations have been avoided and details omitted which would have needlessly overloaded the discussion.

This study relies heavily on secondary sources and relegates economic and technical aspects of the project to second place. In spite of these drawbacks, it is hoped that it can provide a useful overview of the development of the Moselle. The study is chronological rather than topical, and is divided into five time periods delimited by certain key dates in European history. The discussion starts with the *Geography* of Strabo and terminates with some considerations regarding the latest traffic developments on the canalized Moselle River.

---

11 For example, another method would be the comparative analysis of two major transport routes during a given segment of time, as shown in Cermakian, "La Moselle canalisée et la voie maritime du Saint-Laurent: notes comparatives," *Cahiers de Géographie de Québec* 11, no. 23 (1967): 253-74.

II
Early Canalization Projects
(A.D. 58-1792)

The Moselle River is only one of a great number of medium-sized inland waterways which criss-cross the map of northwestern Europe. The layout of this network is so convenient that it has permitted the movement of goods and people since the earliest times. In the first century A.D., the Greek geographer Strabo had already emphasized the ease with which the waterways of Gaul could be used in conjunction with the crossing of low land divides between their headwaters: "The riverbeds are by nature so well situated with reference to one another that there is transportation from either sea into the other; for the cargoes are transported only a short distance by land, with an easy transit through plains, but most of the way they are carried on the rivers — on some into the interior, on the others to the sea."[1]

After their conquest of Gaul, the Romans had also become aware of the need for good communications. That is the reason they founded Lugdunum (Lyons) and made it their entrepôt for northern European trade. The early growth of Lyons was largely due to its location at the Rhône-Saône confluence; from the Saône River, goods were easily transshipped to the Seine and Moselle, whose sources are close to that of the Saône. Lyons thus became the hub of Roman transcontinental trade.

---

1 *The Geography of Strabo,* transl. by H.L. Jones (Cambridge and London: Cambridge University Press, 1960), Book IV, Vol. 2, Ch. I, par. 2, p. 167 (the Loeb edition).

The first project to canalize the Moselle was initiated in 58 A.D., the fourth year of Nero's reign, when all of Gaul was under Roman rule and the Roman *limes* extended to the Rhine and beyond. The Roman historian Tacitus, in his *Annals,* tells us what happened. The governor of Lower Germany, Pompeius Paulinus, to keep the troops busy during that period of relative peace, had them finish the flood-control dikes along the Rhine begun 63 years previously by Nero Drusus. At the same time, the governor of Upper Germany, Lucius Antistius Vetus, embarked on a plan to build a Moselle-Saône canal. Goods travelling from the Mediterranean up the Rhône and Saône would thus go through the Moselle to the Rhine valley, and thence to the North Sea. This would lessen the cost of land transport which proved until then rather prohibitive in financial terms.

Downstream from Augusta Trevirorum (present-day name: Trier in German, Trèves in French), the Moselle served as a boundary between Upper and Lower Germany; its upper section was located in Belgian Gaul. Tacitus informs us that Vetus had to bring his troops into Belgian Gaul, whose governor, Aelius Gracilis, prevented Vetus from doing so, out of envy, arguing that this action might bring Vetus the esteem of the Gauls but that it would also arouse Nero's jealousy. This kind of argument, concludes Tacitus, "often blocks good projects."[2] In this case, the result was that the project was never carried through, even though it would have been a vital strategic and economic link for the Romans.

Well-known as this episode of the Moselle's history might be, it remained for the Gallo-Roman poet Decimus Magnus Ausonius (310-395) to immortalize the river in his descriptive poem, *Mosella.* A native of Burdigala (Bordeaux), Ausonius taught rhetoric and grammar there. Emperor Valentinian chose him as tutor for his son Gratian in 365. At that time, the seat of the Empire was Augusta Trevirorum, so that for nearly 20 years (until the death of Gratian in 383), Ausonius lived there. He was very much appreciated by both emperors, and was made count, quaestor, prefect of Gaul, and imperial consul successively. His most famous work, the poem *Mosella,* was written in 371.[3]

Ausonius paints a very bucolic picture of the way of life in the Moselle valley. He speaks about "the tops of the villas standing out above the overhanging banks, the hills green with vines," describes the rich aquatic fauna of the river by enumerating 15 species of fish, and talks about the oar-driven boat races. He lavishes his praise upon the high-quality vineyards and upon the palatial mansions overlooking the river.

2 Cornelius Tacitus, *The Annals of Imperial Rome,* Book XIII, transl. by Michael Grant (Harmondsworth: Penguin Books, 1956), p. 299.
3 Decimus Magnus Ausonius, *Mosella*, transl. by F.S. Flint (London: 1916), p. 1; and A. Sprunck, "Decimus Magnus Ausonius und seine Moseldichtung," *La Moselle: son passé, son avenir* (Luxembourg: Imprimerie Bourg-Bourger, 1958), pp. 127-8.

As described by Ausonius, life in the Moselle valley was happy and peaceful during the second half of the fourth century. It is no wonder, then, that the emperors had chosen to establish their capital at Augusta Trevirorum, in the midst of this country of plenty. But even though Ausonius stressed the more romantic qualities of the Moselle, he did not fail to draw his readers' attention to the considerable advantage of navigation on the river. Speaking of the latter, the poet exclaimed: "You carry ships like a sea."[4] He further stressed the great importance of river traffic in both directions, mentioning that downbound navigation required nothing but to follow the river current, whereas upbound navigation required paddling and towing.

A recent article seems to contradict Ausonius on the question of navigation techniques, contending that boats going upstream were drawn by horses, not by boatmen, and that those going downstream were towed by boatmen walking along the bank, instead of being rowed.[5] Both kinds of techniques were probably used, depending upon slope, discharge, and stream velocity at any given season and on any given stretch of the river, although this is by no means made clear by the author of the article. At any rate, the Moselle was a major transport route during the Roman period.

For the Romans, the importance of the Moselle was both strategic and economic. As a strategic route at the height of Roman power, it greatly facilitated the transport of troops and supplies towards the garrisons on the Rhine. From the third to the fifth centuries A.D., as Roman power began to decline and finally collapsed, the Rhine and the Vosges Mountains could no longer be held as the Empire's northern boundary and line of defense. The Romans then proceeded to the construction of a line of forts along the Moselle (witness the ruins at Toul, Liverdun, and Pont-à-Mousson, among others). The role of these forts was a) to serve as a rampart for the protection of river traffic (which included the transport of arms, ammunition, and supplies to and between the forts themselves), b) to form a network of relays for signals sent from the Metz headquarters, and c) to be used as base camps for military expeditions against the "barbarians" who were threatening Roman towns and other settlements in border regions.

However important the strategic function of the Moselle may have been, it never really overshadowed the vital commercial role of the river during the Roman period. At that time, traffic on the Moselle River was the monopoly of the *Nautae mosellici* (Moselle boatmen) guild. The economic power of this group

---

4 This was erroneously translated as "navigable like the sea" by F.S. Flint in Ausonius, *Mosella*, p. 3.

5 Heinrich Casper, "Moselschiffahrt im Spiegel der Zeit" (German/French), *Der Ausbau der Mosel/L'aménagement de la Moselle* (hereafter referred to by its French title only) (Trier: SIM, 1966), p. 72.

is reflected by a Roman inscription discovered in the foundations of a church near Metz three centuries ago. It reads as follows: *Marco Publicio Secundano, nautarum mosallicorum liberto tabulario* ("to Marcus Publicius Secundanus, freedman, treasurer of the Moselle boatmen").[6] The Secundanus family was apparently quite powerful in managing the affairs of the boatmen's guild, since its name also appears on a second-century funereal column found at Igel, near Trier.

Funereal steles and monuments erected in the Moselle valley during the second and third centuries A.D. also show the kinds of products transported on the river in those times. The Igel column pictures a barge loaded with bales of cloth and towed by slaves. The funereal stele discovered at Neumagen, 40 km downstream from Trier, depicts a large rowing-boat loaded with wine casks (Plate 1).[7] These products of the Moselle valley – wine and cloth – were shipped southward to Italy via the Saône and Lyons. In exchange, the cities of Metz and Trier received various goods from southern Gaul, Spain, and more distant regions of the Empire: olive oil, fruit, earthenwares, among others. There was also a sizable trade in construction materials; large volumes of building stone from quarries located on the left bank near Metz were shipped down the Moselle to the Rhine valley to be used in sculptures, monuments, and houses. In return, blocks of basalt used in the construction of the Roman bridge at Trier, and granite columns for the Trier cathedral, were shipped from the Odenwald region of west-central Germany.

All this active trade took place during the imperial period, after the founding of Augusta Trevirorum (ca. 15 B.C.). It is not clear to what extent the military operations which took place during the latter part of this period interfered with commercial traffic on the river. Nor is it clear how far south the Moselle was navigable, and there are no indications of the physical characteristics of the river except for the rather vague words of Ausonius about its gentle slope and peaceful waters. Moreover, there are no precise descriptions of the craft used during this period; the above-mentioned archeological evidence merely indicates the existence of large rowing-boats and of flat-bottomed barges towed by men or horses. Finally, no mention is made of passenger traffic, but it must be assumed that the excellent network of Roman highways provided adequately for such movement.

In the final analysis, during the Roman period, and down to the present, the prosperity of navigation on the Moselle River and the economic health of the neighboring regions have been determined by the evolution of attitudes towards the river: "Thus, the dual vocation of the Moselle became apparent 1,900 years

6 Albert Houpert, *La Moselle navigable: des Nautae gallo-romains au CAMIFEMO* (Metz: Chambre de Commerce de Metz, 1932), p. 3. (Author's transl.)
7 Léon Hild, "Deux millénaires de navigation mosellane," *RNIR* **36** (1964): 377.

Plate 1 Roman rowing-boat on the Moselle River, loaded with wine casks. Reproduction of a third-century A.D. funereal stele, Neumagen, Rheinland-Pfalz, West Germany. The original stele is kept in the Trier City Museum. Author's photograph, 22 April 1965.

ago: that of a great transportation route laid out by nature, and at the same time that of an eternal victim of political quarrels and rivalries. Navigation on it flourished or declined, depending upon which of these two characteristics prevailed."[8]

MEDIEVAL TRADE ON THE MOSELLE

There is a scarcity of documents concerning the period which followed the collapse of the Roman Empire. It is known, however, that Metz and Thionville, once flourishing Roman towns, were also the birthplaces of the Carolingian Empire. Charlemagne's ancestor, St Arnould, swept away the last remnants of Roman administration and became bishop of Metz in 613. He had put an end to the rule of the Austrasian kings, successors of the Romans, whose palace was at

8 Robert Vadot, "La navigation sur la Moselle française dans le passé et dans l'avenir" (French/German) in *L'aménagement de la Moselle* (Trier: SIM, 1966), p. 79.

Metz and who used the Moselle River for travel and pleasure. One such journey had been undertaken by the sixth-century poet and superior of the Poitiers abbey, Venantius Fortunatus.[9]

Even though Roman rule as such had ended, Roman tradition was still very strong in the Carolingian Empire. The latter had a strong central authority and was very active in the defense and propagation of the Christian faith. Charlemagne even tried to maintain the Roman highway network by appointing special public works commissioners for this purpose. But this task was made difficult by the increasing number of tolls levied by local lords on the Empire's roads. Charlemagne himself preferred to travel by boat on the Moselle between the palaces of Remiremont, Metz, Thionville, and other places in or near the Moselle valley. There is no documentary evidence of trade on the river during this period, although Metz, as one of the main cities of the Empire, must have been an important trade center.

Charlemagne's Empire was partitioned in 843 by his three grandsons. One of them, Lothar, received the central kingdom, or Lotharingia (Lorraine), bounded to the east by the Rhine and to the west by the "limit of the four rivers" (Scheldt, Meuse, Saône, and Rhône). The Moselle thus became the central axis of the new kingdom. But the latter did not survive feudal quarrels, and by the mid-tenth century, Lotharingia had been partitioned among many rulers, most of whom were (at least in theory) vassals of the Holy Roman Germanic Emperor. The course of the Moselle thus ran through the Duchies of Lorraine and Luxembourg, the County of Bar, the Archbishopric of Trier, and the Bishoprics of Metz, Toul, Verdun, and Koblenz: "it had been internationalized by the feudal powers."[10] Feudalism, far from hampering navigation on the Moselle, encouraged it, because with the decline of the road network, the importance of navigable waterways kept on increasing.

Trier, the former capital of the Roman Empire, had become the seat of an important Archbishopric-Electorate during the Middle Ages. The Archbishop of Trier was a political power to be reckoned with in the Holy Roman Empire. Given the poor condition of the roads, the archbishops maintained a large fleet of riverboats for their travels. According to medieval chroniclers, Albero, Archbishop of Trier from 1131 to 1152, once travelled to the Imperial Diet in Frankfurt with a convoy of 40 ships followed by numerous messenger launches and supply barges.

Medieval Trier also inherited the commercial tradition of the Gallo-Roman *Nautae mosellici.* The shipping guilds founded in 1252 included both the citizens who owned the river craft and the boatmen who operated them. One of these

9 Marcel Grosdidier de Matons, introduction to Houpert, *La Moselle navigable,* pp. v-vi.
10 *Ibid.,* p. vi. (Author's transl.)

guilds, the St Paul shipping brotherhood, was still in existence in 1927, after 675 years of continuous operation. The statutes of these guilds were very strictly enforced and were therefore greatly respected. They included provisions against corrupt business and labor practices and unfair competition, and dealt with the establishment of freight rates and conditions of chartering.

In addition to shipping guilds, there was one other means of transportation on the Moselle: the so-called *Marktschiffe* (market boats). These, unlike guild craft, sailed on regular schedules and carried goods and passengers alike with no restrictions. They were usually operated by the Elector of Trier and by the rulers of other towns along the Moselle. There is an instance of a *Marktschiff* being built for the city of Trier in 1373. Some *Marktschiff* operations were granted to individual boatmen who had to sail on a regular basis, especially on market days.[11]

The commercial importance of Trier as a great river port during the Middle Ages may further be understood when one looks at the imposing crane built in 1413 and still standing on the riverbank today (Plate 2).

The main reason for the commercial prosperity of Metz was also political. During the Middle Ages, even though a part of the Holy Roman Empire, Metz was ruled by a bishop and enjoyed almost complete autonomy from the Duke of Lorraine's authority. It was often referred to as *la République messine* (the Metz Republic). Under these circumstances, and due to the business ability of its bourgeois-merchant class, commerce flourished.[12]

Metz was second only to Cologne in importance as a trade center in the Empire. One of the city's oldest river embankments, the present-day *Quai de l'Arsenal,* was known as *Rim-port* (Rhine port) during the thirteenth century. The great volume of goods handled there account for the enormous warehouses which were built along the riverbank at that time. The floors of these buildings were supported by a great number of beams resting upon large wooden pillars; there were no interior walls or partitions to interrupt the floor space, which was used mostly for the temporary storage of incoming wheat or wool. From the north, and the Rhine valley in particular, the chief imports were wool and leather, both of which were in great demand as raw materials for the city's leatherwork and textile industries. From the north also came Cologne iron, chalk, mill-stones, linens, furs, and oil. This traffic was carried out by foreign boatmen, mostly Dutch, some Flemish. From the southern parts of Lorraine, salt was shipped down the Moselle and its tributaries, the Meurthe and the Seille,

---

11 Johann Baptist Keune, *Moselschiffahrt in alter und neuer Zeit: Festschrift zur Erinnerung an das 675-Jährige Bestehen der Schifferbruderschaft Trier-St. Paulus* (Trier: 1927), quoted in Houpert, *La Moselle navigable.*
12 Roland Nistri et Claude Prêcheur, *La région du Nord/Nord-Est* (Paris: Presses Universitaires de France, 1959), p. 32.

Plate 2 The medieval crane at Trier, West Germany. Built in 1413 on the bank of the Moselle River, this watch-tower-like masonry structure still stands in a good state of repair. Author's photograph, 22 April 1965.

to Metz. The city also received wine from Beaune (Burgundy), which came up the Saône and was transhipped by land over the divide to the Moselle. Finally, there is evidence of passenger traffic, including pilgrims who travelled free of charge.

This prosperity was bound to create some rivalry with the city-state's neighbors: in 1483, the Governor of Luxembourg seized some craft on the Moselle belonging to the citizens of Metz, and in 1488, the latter complained that some of their vessels had been stopped by the Archbishop of Trier's men on la franche rivière de Moselle (the free Moselle River). But these incidents were infrequent. More often the Moselle between Metz and Trier was used for travel by high officials and dignitaries. Emperor Charles of Bohemia went from Metz to Thionville in 1356; the Archbishop of Strasbourg made a journey from Metz to Trier in 1492, involving two large vessels and 60 people and lasting two days.[13]

13 E.-A. Bégin, *Histoire des Sciences, des Lettres, des Arts et de la civilisation dans le Pays messin depuis les Gaulois jusqu'à nos jours* (Metz: 1829), pp. 300 and 339-40, quoted in Houpert, *La Moselle navigable.*

The sixteenth century was one of continued prosperity for Trier, one of mixed fortunes for Metz. There is only one instance of active trade involving Metz during this period: timber floating began, especially from the upper reaches of the Moselle around Remiremont (i.e., from the fir forests of the Vosges Mountains), downstream to Metz. This traffic is said to have been active throughout the sixteenth century and for the first 35 years of the seventeenth; then, it gradually dwindled to nothing around 1700.

The main reason for the decline of Metz was that the free city had become a bone of contention between France and the Empire. In 1552, France occupied les Trois-Evêchés (the Three Bishoprics) of Metz, Toul, and Verdun, and thus consolidated its line of defense against the Empire by establishing three outposts within the latter's territory. This occupation followed the worsening of relations between Metz and its neighbors to the point of open hostilities and, together with the city's involvement in the wars of religion, led to the steady decline of urban growth and the dwindling of river trade. The focus of commercial activity in northwestern Europe now definitely shifted to the Rhine valley.

On the other hand, the city of Trier retained its political and commercial importance throughout the sixteenth century. In 1512, Emperor Maximilian I travelled up the Moselle to attend a meeting of the Imperial Diet which took place there. Commercial traffic on the river was intense. The *Marktschiffe* carried passengers and freight from Trier to the Frankfurt Trade Fair on several occasions. Other Moselle craft made frequent trips to Cologne, Mainz, Mannheim, and Heidelberg, via the Rhine and Neckar rivers. The main products transported had not changed much since the Roman period: wine still topped the list, followed by building materials and salt; coal and iron traffic had appeared during the Middle Ages.

In the medieval period no project seems to have been initiated for the improvement or canalization of the Moselle. Although no records exist concerning the matter, it is likely that a minimum depth of channel was maintained at all times, at least until the mid-sixteenth century. Thereafter, the river seems to have been allowed to silt gradually, so that by 1700 it had become all but useless for navigation upstream of Metz.

Prosperity of trade and traffic on the river was a result of political stability. Even after the breakup of the Carolingian Empire, the great many feudal powers who shared sovereignty over the Moselle were willing to "internationalize" the river and maintain freedom of navigation for the benefit of everyone concerned. This was the age of toll-free waterways, of flourishing city-States, and of great trade fairs all over Europe. The "umbrella" of German imperial authority was one added factor of stability. When this authority was challenged by the French kings, and when the wars of religion tore northwestern Europe apart, political stability disappeared, and with it trade, prosperity, and urban growth.

With the disintegration of the Roman road network, inland navigation had also become the safest and fastest means of transport and consequently a powerful instrument of political control for emperors and other rulers. This factor accounts for the innumerable travels of high officials mentioned earlier. The large fleets of river craft used for this purpose had become one of the major institutions in medieval river traffic.

Political stability and commercial prosperity also gave rise to other institutions: the shipping guilds, which were the direct inheritors of the *Nautae mosellici* tradition, and whose statutes were rigidly enforced; and the publicly-owned *Marktschiffe,* which were forerunners of regularly scheduled passenger and freight riverboat services.

In many ways, the institutions and practices of medieval navigation on the Moselle were the reflection of a golden age for international trade. The basic principles of free navigation proclaimed by the French Revolution in 1792 were a result of the abuses and excesses of transport policies established by the absolute monarchies of the seventeenth and eighteenth centuries. But the roots of these principles ran deep into medieval tradition, during a period which saw the establishment and expansion of the Hanseatic fleets in the river and seaports of northwestern Europe.

CANALIZATION PROJECTS IN THE SEVENTEENTH AND
EIGHTEENTH CENTURIES

Rivalries between local rulers, wars of religion, and the confrontation between France and the Holy Roman Empire during the sixteenth century had hampered the progress of navigation on the Moselle and interrupted it several times. The Thirty Years' War (1618-48) and the military campaigns of Louis XIV during the second half of the seventeenth century put a virtual end to all commercial traffic on the river. Most of the riverboats were requisitioned to carry troops, ammunition, and supplies to the battlefields. For example, Louis XIV had most of his war supplies transported on the Moselle and Rhine in the campaign against Holland.

In 1648, the Treaty of Westphalia proclaimed freedom of navigation on all the major European rivers, including the Moselle. But this principle was respected for a short time only, and the river trade did not recover from its wartime slump. The main reason was that the electors, princes, bishops, and other local rulers, motivated by self-interest, imposed tolls and transit duties on all river traffic, thereby invalidating the free navigation clauses of the 1648 treaty. This situation was well described by Jacques-Etienne Turgot, Intendant (Governor) of the Province of Metz from 1696 to 1700, in a 1699 report he wrote by command of Louis XIV. Downstream from Metz, the river was so heavily burdened with tolls that a commodity shipped from Metz to the Rhine valley had doubled in price by the time it reached its destination. There were

A. *Paulinus*. B. *S. Maximin*. C. *Simeon*. D. *Nigra porta*. E. *S. Martin*. F. *Deutfchhaus*. G. *Dom kirch*. H. *Vnfer Er aw en*. I

Plate 3 The Moselle River at Trier in 1646. From a Matthaeus Merian print, published in *Topographia Archiepiscopatuum Moguntinensis, Treuirensis et Coloniensis* (Trier: 1646), and reproduced from a 1965 calendar.

tolls even in the king's domain, at Thionville, Cattenom, and Sierck, four more in Luxembourg, and many more in the Electorate of Trier and the principalities further downstream. This made the river totally uneconomical, and the only goods which could pay their way through the numerous toll barriers were extremely expensive commodities such as wheat occasionally shipped from Frankfurt-am-Main. Upstream from Metz, the obstacles to navigation were physical rather than economic: the river was dammed in many places (even

22

olph. K. Palatium. L. Albaporta. M. Carthus. N. Alte Ruine. O. S. Barbara. P. S. Matthias.

within the city of Metz), so that its waterfalls could be used by flour mills and various other industries located along the riverbanks.[14] Here is one of the first pieces of evidence concerning conflicts of interest on the Moselle between water power and navigation.

14 Jacques-Etienne Turgot, *Mémoires historiques de la Lorraine et des Trois-Evêchés* (Bibliothèque de Metz, MS 249: 1699), quoted in Houpert, *La Moselle navigable.*

23

Under these circumstances, few improvement or canalization projects could have had any success. The famous marshal, fortress-builder, and military strategist, Vauban, studied the possibilities of a Moselle-Meuse link near Toul in 1658 (Figure 2).[15]

Vauban's idea was to build a Moselle-Meuse canal from Toul to Pagny-sur-Meuse, a distance of about 20 km, utilizing for that purpose the water of two small tributaries of the Meuse and Moselle flowing in opposite directions and separated by a low, narrow divide. The canal would be fed by a small ditch, 15-18 feet wide, 2-3 feet deep, which would collect the surplus stream water of one drainage basin and supply it to the other, after having crossed the divide through a 3000-foot long cut. The canal itself would follow a route parallel to the courses of the two brooks, and would be about 40 feet wide and 6 feet deep. There is no mention of how many locks would be necessary on this canal, and what the dimensions of those locks should be. On the other hand, Vauban emphasized the need for dredging the Meuse from Pagny to St Mihiel and the Moselle from Epinal to Frouard, building a great number of sluice gates on both rivers (here we have the first hint of a need for canalization), and a lateral canal along the Moselle at Toul, including one lock chamber and two bridges overhead for the benefit of the city's commerce and industries.

Vauban appealed to the rulers of Luxembourg, Trier, Bar, and Lorraine (especially the latter) and made it clear that it would be in the best interest of all concerned to increase their trade with France through this link. This would be all the easier since the Ardennes Canal, under construction at that time, would link the Meuse and the Seine via the Aisne and Oise rivers. The chief product of trade would have been fir timber from the Vosges Mountains, which could be floated down the Meurthe and Moselle. This timber could serve many purposes, principally shipbuilding and the construction of houses. Other trade items would have included firewood from around St Mihiel and Toul, slate, iron, flax, dairy products from the Vosges valleys, coal, wheat, oats, and hay from the Lorraine valleys.

However, Vauban was a soldier and as such his chief interest lay in the strategic value of the projected link. The latter would allow French strongholds in the Meuse and Moselle valleys to be supplied from Lorraine. Moreover, it would facilitate the movement of troops in any future campaign, since the greater part of the proposed route was located in the king's domain. But campaigns were expensive, and there were no funds available to finance Vauban's spectacular project.

The military importance of inland navigation was also apparent in the project conceived by P.E. de Mansfeld to link Luxembourg with the Moselle River.

---

15 Vauban's 1658 project was finally carried out in 1853, when the Marne-Rhine Canal linked Pagny on the Meuse with Toul on the Moselle.

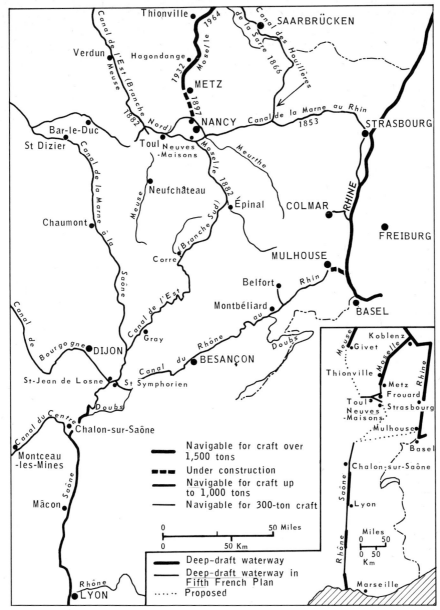

Figure 2 The Moselle River in the waterways network of northeastern France. Draft status as of 1974. The main map also shows construction dates of some of the waterways discussed in the text. The inset (bottom right) is a diagram of the three alternate Mediterranean-to-North Sea waterway links also discussed in the text.

Louis XIV, after occupying the city of Luxembourg, had it fortified, and the need was great for fast communications with other French forts to the south. The proposed route would have followed the Alzette River southward for about 8 km to Roeser, and from there a canal would have been built due eastward to the Moselle across the escarpment overlooking the west bank of the river. Another alternative was to cut a canal through the divide between the Alzette and Syr rivers, and follow the latter, which flows into the Moselle at Mertert. Mansfeld's project was seriously considered several times during the following centuries, but was never carried out. Two of the many reasons for this were the high cost of construction and the frequent changes in political control over Luxembourg which made any such long-range project hazardous to undertake. Moreover, no economic justification could be given in this case, as it had been in Vauban's project.

During the first 15 years of the eighteenth century, the Moselle was still primarily used for military transport. The campaigns of Louis XIV against Holland and the Palatinate required the use of this fast supply route. In 1701, for example, numerous barge convoys departed from Metz towards Koblenz and Pont-à-Mousson, the former to supply the troops besieging Trarbach and Landau (Palatinate), the latter to help maintain the large army corps working on the fortifications of Nancy. Hundreds of barges carried wooden beams, cannons, ammunition, fodder, food supplies, etc., to the far-flung outposts and battlefields. Five years later, combined land-river military maneuvers between Metz and Thionville also created an intense river traffic. The Moselle had thus become an effective instrument of military policy.

At the same time, however, the repeated wars and campaigns had gradually put an end to all commercial traffic on the river. As a result, the formerly great trading centers, Metz and Trier, were now but shadows of their medieval past: the population of Metz had fallen to one-tenth its former size and poverty had become extreme. In many places, the river had become so clogged with silt that it was almost useless for navigation. Nevertheless, with the return of peace, some commercial traffic had resumed by the middle of the century, in spite of the great number of tolls and the physical obstacles in the riverbed. There is evidence, during this period, of trade in the following items: metal products shipped from the ironworks at Moyeuvre and Hayange (Lorraine) to the Rhine valley, Burgundy wines transported via the Moselle to the Principality of Liège, rapeseed from Lorraine shipped to Holland, where it was converted to oil for use in ships and linen industries, and salt from the mines at Rosières (near Frouard) shipped down the Meurthe and Moselle to Metz. Finally, some of the timber trade, which had been flourishing during the sixteenth century, was revived. The logs were usually carted to a point on the Moselle downstream from Epinal, and thence floated down river to Pont-à-Mousson, Metz, and Koblenz. The chief customers in this trade were the Dutch, who often re-exported the timber to

France as a "product of the northern forests." However, the Dutch preferred to use the Saar River in this trade, because it was not burdened with as many tolls as the Moselle. Moreover, in this case, they themselves went to the Vosges and converted the timber into shipmasts before floating the latter down river. On the other hand, the French floated the shipmasts down the Moselle as far as Toul, carted them overland from Toul to Bar-le-Duc, and from there rafted them down the Ornain, Marne, and Seine rivers to Le Havre.[16]

But all this traffic represented a mere fraction of what it once had been at the height of the prosperous medieval trade. Nevertheless, navigation on the lower Moselle River went through a period of brief prosperity in the eighteenth century. The upper section of the Rhine being poorly maintained, barges carrying goods bound for Basle would travel up the Moselle as far as Trier; from there, they were carted overland to their destination via Saarbrücken and Strasbourg. This temporary prosperity had also been made possible as a result of a conference held in 1717 at Bacharach by the Electors of Mainz, Cologne, Trier, and the Palatinate, at which the solution to a number of problems concerning inland navigation within their respective States were worked out in common. River traffic still offered considerable advantages over road transport at that time, and had to be encouraged; but no mention was made of tolls and other duties at this conference.

In 1769, the Société Royale des Sciences et Arts de Metz (Metz Royal Society of Sciences and Arts) decided to organize a contest for the best reports to be written in answer to the following question: "Quels sont les obstacles physiques et politiques qui s'opposent à la navigation, non seulement de la rivière de Moselle, mais encore dans les autres rivières principales de la province (des Trois-Evêchés)?" (What are the physical and political obstacles which stand in the way of navigation, not only on the Moselle River, but also on the other major rivers of the Province [of the Three Bishoprics]?).[17]

The contest and studies were under the sponsorship of Monsieur de Calonne, Intendant (Governor) of the Province. The prize-winning reports were read in public hearings at the Société Royale in 1772, and analyzed conditions as of that date. The prize for the report on political obstacles and on the means to remove the latter went to a Monsieur Blouet, Avocat en Parlement (barrister in the High Court) in Metz.

The first part of the Blouet report dealt with existing and potential river trade in the Province. The nature of the existing export trade has already been

16 T.C.C. Boissel, *Voyage pittoresque et navigation exécutée sur une partie du Rhône réputée non-navigable* ... (Paris: Imprimerie Nationale, Year III of the Republic, i.e., 1795), p. 3.
17 Bibliothèque de Metz, MS 994 (1772), quoted in Houpert, *La Moselle navigable.* (Author's transl.)

discussed. Its main customers were the Dutch, who were primarily interested in timber and rapeseed, and who preferred to use the Saar River over the Moselle, the latter being too heavily burdened with tolls. Exports to Germany included only occasional shipments of Burgundy wines, cloth, and some luxury items. In sharp contrast to the rather bleak export situation, imports from Holland included a great variety of items: sugar, spices, dyes, drugs, fish, tropical foodstuffs and beverages, and paper products. Imports from Germany included Moselle and Rhine wines, mineral water, coal, earthenwares, and slate. The balance of trade was thus extremely unfavorable for Metz. Moreover, the entrepôt function of the city had all but disappeared, except for some re-export to Lorraine of fish and spices imported from Holland. Most of the entrepôt trade had been taken over by Lorraine and Saar merchants. Finally, in domestic trade, the province imported enormous amounts of manufactured goods from Paris and Lyons, with no goods to give in return. The net result of this situation was a massive outflow of cash towards these cities, barely balanced by the income derived from the Metz garrison. But the latter had been drastically reduced since the end of the long series of wars and military campaigns of the seventeenth and early eighteenth centuries. This left the city and its trade in a worse condition than ever.

Part of the problem was that, even though the Three Bishoprics had been annexed by France in 1552, the Thionville district in 1659, and the Duchies of Bar and Lorraine in 1766, many foreign enclaves remained within the newly acquired territories until the French Revolution. Moreover, the former customs boundaries between France, the Three Bishoprics, and Lorraine remained even after annexation. It is true that many of the products of these areas required customs protection: for example, wine from the Metz region, one of its chief resources, could not survive in open competition with Champagne or Burgundy wines. This paradoxical customs situation also meant that the Province of the Three Bishoprics was treated as foreign by the French authorities as well as by all its other neighbors.

Under these circumstances, any attempt to expand the already well-established local industries (such as those based on flax or hemp) in order to foster trade would prove unsuccessful in the face of foreign (especially Belgian) competition. So the only valid role left for the Moselle in general, and for Metz in particular, would be that of an entrepôt center for trade between southern France, Spain, and Italy on the one hand, and southwestern Germany on the other. Metz could import rice, vegetable oils, soap, wine, dried fruit, and spirits from the south and re-export them to Lorraine, Alsace, Basle, Saarbrücken, Trier, the Palatinate, the Rhineland, Baden, and Wurtemberg. This would not necessarily mean that the Moselle region could hold a monopoly of trade to and from those States, but at least it could have a share of it, re-establishing the role of eastern France as a major transit route between the Mediterranean and north-western Europe. This role had been lost in 1585 when King Henry III of France had established prohibitive transit duties on foreign goods moving through Lyons; as a result, English, Dutch, and Flemish ships eventually gained almost complete control of the Mediterranean-to-North Sea trade.

The major obstacle to navigation on the Moselle, however, and a by-product of this political situation, was the incredible number of tolls and duties levied on the river itself. These were discussed at length in the second part of the Blouet report. The toll levied at Thionville was a survival of the customs duty levied there on river traffic before 1643, when Thionville was part of the Duchy of Luxembourg, then under Austrian rule. Since it had been annexed by France, no royal assent had been given to the collection of any such duty, which was therefore illegal. A few miles downstream, at Cattenom, the local lord levied another toll. In this case, a royal ordinance allowed such collection only for the purpose of encouraging trade by the maintenance of a deep navigation channel and the provision of public safety; but there was no evidence that the lord of Cattenom had honored his obligations. The third collection point was at Sierck, a town which had belonged to the Duke of Lorraine until 1661, when it had been yielded to France. It was near the border with Luxembourg, and was therefore a customs collection point for all goods entering Lorraine. By a series of agreements, those goods bound for Metz were admitted duty-free, and this was still the case under French rule in 1759, when a new local ruler decided to extend all the duties levied previously on Lorraine-bound goods only to traffic bound for the Three Bishoprics. Not content with this action, he quadrupled these duties at the same time, thus exceeding the rights granted to him by royal privilege. As a result, Metz-bound traffic on the Moselle dwindled and was diverted either through the Saar valley and thence to Metz by land, or from Grevenmacher through Luxembourg and down to Metz, also by land. In spite of all the costly break-in-bulk transfers, these routes were less expensive to use than the Moselle through Sierck.

The next toll was collected at Remich (Luxembourg). During the Middle Ages, several treaties between the Metz Republic and the Counts of Luxembourg had established free navigation on the Moselle between the two States. This status was reconfirmed in 1599 by the Austrian Archduke who then ruled Luxembourg, but lost during the Franco-Austrian wars of the following century when the extremely high Remich tariff had been established. In spite of several reductions in the latter from 1765 on, it was still the highest duty levied on the Moselle outside France.

There were several more tolls to be paid on the Moselle in the Electorate of Trier. The duties at Trier were collected by the city rather than by the elector. There was a duty to be paid for the privilege of sailing under the bridge, and a transit duty, known as Stapel Gerechtigkeit, which the citizens of Trier claimed was derived from a privilege granted to them by Emperor Otto IV in the thirteenth century. One of its features was the right, in times of want, to hold all boats carrying grain, firewood, and coal for 3 days so that the inhabitants might take advantage of these supplies at the lowest possible prices. But such practice led to abuses even during more prosperous times, to the greater advantage of Trier's merchants who could thus make handsome profits, and to the dismay of the boatmen who underwent severe losses.

The three tolls levied in the Electorate of Trier downstream from that city (at Pfalzel, Cochem, and Koblenz) were more moderate. The rate of these tolls was set through bargaining sessions between local officials and boatmen. But even though toll collection was one of the elector's chief sources of income, and could therefore not be eliminated, bilateral negotiations between France and the Electorate, in order to reduce the tolls, could be carried out for the benefit of boatmen in both states.

The great number of tolls levied on the Moselle was not the only major political obstacle to trade. The other one was the nature of these tolls. Most states based their toll rates on the volume or weight of goods carried, rather than on their value. Since Metz and Lorraine exported mostly low per-unit value raw materials and semi-finished products, and imported high-value tropical commodities and manufactured goods from Holland and Germany, the nature of the tolls favored the latter countries.

A final deterrent to the commercial prosperity of navigation on the upper Moselle, discussed in the third part of the Blouet report, was the great number of prohibitive taxes and duties, known as maltôtes, imposed by the city of Metz upon imported raw materials, locally-produced manufactured goods, and entrepôt trade commodities. The author recommended the complete elimination of the latter and a sizable reduction in the others, arguing that excessive taxation stifled consumption and ruined the chances of Metz as an entrepôt trade center, the latter role having been taken over by the towns in the Saar valley.

The fourth part of the report dealt with solutions to the existing political problems. The author's first recommendation was to abolish all toll collection points in the province except the one at Sierck, where a single customs duty would be paid on all goods entering the province. Secondly, there was to be a ban on the export of grain and raw materials vital to the local industires, e.g., timber. Other raw materials, such as flax and hemp, could be exported after being charged a small duty. In this case, the cheaper labor costs in the province would make local finished products competitive with those imported from Holland. For all other goods, including wines and manufactured products, not only was there to be no export tax, but exports would have to be encouraged with bonuses and subsidies from the central government. On the other hand, it would be dangerous to charge excessive duties on goods imported from Holland and Germany via Sierck, because:

1 those goods could (and did) travel up the Saar and reach Metz by land;
2 they could come through Nancy, since the free navigation treaty between the Three Bishoprics and Lorraine was still in force;

30

3 they could be transported by road from Frankfurt;
4 the closing of all land and river border crossings between the Moselle and Saar valleys would encourage smuggling, to the greater advantage of the Saar merchants.

Finally, the best way for Metz to become once again the hub of the entrepôt trade between Holland and Germany on the one hand and Lorraine, Alsace, and Switzerland on the other, was to abolish or considerably reduce duties on goods to be re-exported. This would have eliminated the danger of a treaty (being negotiated at that time) between the Dutch and the Saarbrücken merchants, whereby the latter would commit themselves to transport all Dutch goods shipped to Switzerland for a period of 20 years.

Interesting and useful as the Blouet report might have been, it failed to point out the root of the problem, namely the social and political system under which the economic woes of the Moselle valley (and of France as a whole) were allowed to persist. By the 1770s, there had been a great reaction of the nobility to the king's absolute power, and the latter had been seriously shaken. After the wars of Louis XIV, northeastern France and Lorraine had to suffer from a return of feudalism of the worst kind, which meant obstacles to trade and industry in the form of tolls, duties, and unjustified municipal taxes. Nothing could change this system short of a revolution.

While political obstacles were difficult to remove, physical hindrances to navigation on the Moselle could be eliminated with existing technology, after preliminary studies had been carried out. Some of these were also sponsored by the Société Royale in Metz. The prize-winning report was written by Gardeur-Lebrun, a civil engineer, who travelled down the Moselle from Metz to Koblenz and back, accompanied by Governor de Calonne. The author of the report also drew up a map of the Moselle valley between Metz and Koblenz which is a model in map-engraving for this period (Plate 4).

The report included eight recommendations for the removal of major physical obstacles to navigation on this section of the Moselle:
1 Of the three bridges spanning the river (at Koblenz, Trier, and Thionville), only the one at Thionville offered any difficulties to boatmen on account of its low headroom. But it was up to the boatmen themselves to fold their masts down to the deck, an operation which would cause them only a very slight delay. This was certainly a more economical solution than doing work on the bridge.
2 Fifty-five islands were counted in the river channel, but only three of these (at Kues, Neumagen, and Pölich) caused problems for navigation. In most cases, the boat channel was located between the island and the riverbank on which the tow-path was located. In the three above-mentioned islands, the tow-path was located on the island bank. Therefore, the tow-horses had to cross the river from

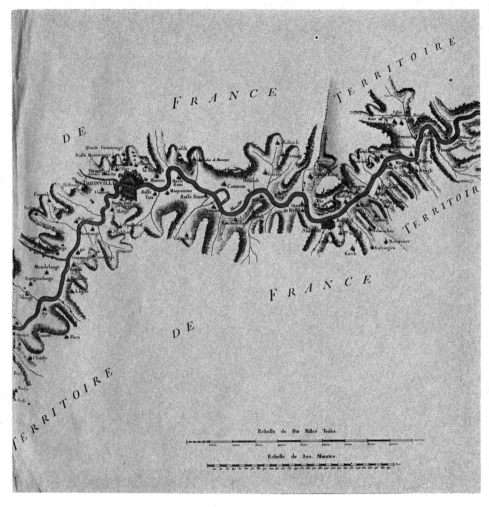

Plate 4 Fragment of Gardeur-Lebrun's map of the Moselle valley (1772), reproduced in Martin Gerges, ed., *La Moselle: Son passé, son avenir* (Schwebsingen:
1958).

the riverbank to the island, often at a great risk. In such cases, tow-paths would
have to be built on the riverbank side of the boat channel.
3 There were also 31 sand and gravel banks in the riverbed. Some of these
would have to be dredged out completely, others only within the confines of the
boat channel. Some could even be carried away by the river's flow if the riverbed
were narrowed artificially by building groins perpendicular to the riverbank, or
fascines along the same.

32

III
Free Navigation and the Nation-States (1792-1871)

THE PRINCIPLE OF FREE NAVIGATION

We have seen that the idea of free navigation had been embodied in many unwritten and formal agreements among feudal States during the Middle Ages. In the period which followed, the principle was destroyed and river traffic became just another source of tax and customs revenues. The final turning point came with the proclamation of the Principle of Free Navigation in a decree of the Provisional Executive Council of the French Republic on 16 November 1792. The terms of the decree read as follows: "River courses are the common and unalienable property of all the regions through which they flow. A nation cannot justly claim the exclusive right to control a river channel and to prevent the neighboring peoples who occupy the upper reaches from enjoying the same advantages."[1]

In effect, the proclamation meant that there was to be equal treatment of foreigners on any country's waterways, that transit duties and tolls would have to be abolished, and that national transport legislations would have to be harmonized for the benefit of all carriers, regardless of nationality.

The decree of 1792 abolished all tolls, duties, and taxes levied on river and canal traffic within the boundaries of the French Republic. These boundaries were pushed outward during the ensuing years as a result of the revolutionary wars, so that by 1797 all of Belgium and Luxembourg, the southern provinces of the Netherlands, and all the German principalities located west of the Rhine

---

1 Bonét-Maury, *Les Actes du Rhin et de la Moselle* (3rd. ed., Strasbourg: Les Editions de la Navigation du Rhin, 1966), introduction, p. 6.

had been incorporated into the French Republic. The abolition of tolls and other levies on inland navigation were thus also extended to the Moselle, Rhine, Saar, Meuse, Sambre, and Scheldt rivers.

A report advocating the elimination of tolls on these rivers had been read in 1795 at a meeting of the Metz Municipal Council, at a time when peace negotiations were still underway with Holland, Prussia, and other German princes.[2] The main argument of this report was that since the French government had decided to eliminate tolls on rivers, the other States were expected to do likewise, according to the principle of reciprocity. Secondly, maritime and inland navigation being the easiest and cheapest means of communication between various societies, a ruler who arbitrarily imposed tolls and other duties on river traffic was not only working against good understanding between peoples, but also against his own interests and those of his subjects. Thirdly, whereas high-value, low-weight goods could afford to travel by road, bulky low per-unit value commodities could afford neither road transport nor river navigation if the latter were burdened with excessive tolls. As a result, river traffic stagnated or dwindled, and the expected revenues from tolls could not even pay for the cost of collecting them, let alone bring in a sizable income to the ruler. Finally, freedom of navigation would restore the previous prosperity of the great European trade centers. This prosperity would in turn more than offset the loss in tax revenues which the State would have suffered as a result of the elimination of tolls.

Turning more specifically to the Rhine and Moselle, the report listed and described the 29 toll collection offices still in existence at the time between Rotterdam and Metz: 6 in Holland, 5 in Prussia, 7 in the Electorate of Cologne, 2 in the Palatinate, 6 in the Electorate of Trier, and 3 in the Duchy of Luxembourg. The prohibitive Stapel Gerechtigkeiten (transit duties) levied by the cities of Cologne and Trier were still in existence. The report emphasized that there was no case for negotiating toll reductions or for substituting new duties for existing ones; French occupation of these areas would eliminate duties altogether. What was more important, once the occupied territories were returned to their rulers, the latter would have to agree not to reinstate tolls, duties, or any other obstacles to river traffic and trade. Removal of political obstacles would in turn favor the elimination of those physical obstacles already mentioned. And the report concluded that by removing such artificial causes of jealousy and rivalry among peoples, one would destroy the bases of national hatreds and therefore contribute to the building of peace and friendship among nations.

2 Barbé and Adam, "Observations sur la libre navigation de la Moselle et du Rhin," *Extrait du Registre des Délibérations du Conseil Général de la commune de Metz, du 24 messidor, An 3e de la République Française, une et indivisible* (Metz: Year III of the Republic, i.e., 1795).

Thus, the French Revolution's contribution to the advancement of inland navigation was primarily political. On the technical and economic side, the record was far less commendable. However, in 1799, the French Minister of the Interior, François de Neufchâteau, a native of Lorraine, drew up a plan for a nationwide inland waterways system, including the project for a Rhine-Meurthe-Moselle-Meuse link, a forerunner of the present-day Marne-Rhine Canal, and a reconsideration of the Moselle-Saône link proposed by Lecreulx in 1776. At the same time, the old Mansfeld project for a Luxembourg-Moselle canal was revived, and a petition was sent to the government requesting the authorization to build a canal between Luxembourg and Liège, following the valleys of the Alzette, Sûre, Wiltz, Clerf, and Ourthe rivers through the Ardennes. None of these projects were carried out, but the French did improve navigation conditions on the Moselle, including dredging of sand banks and removal of rocks from the riverbed, repairing of tow-paths and riverbanks, and removal of fish ladders and other obstacles.

Despite the efforts made to remove these obstacles, river traffic did not regain its former importance during this period. In 1805, there was some commercial downbound traffic in wines, timber, coal, lime, gypsum, and some upbound traffic in various goods shipped from Dutch and Rhineland ports. The craft used in this traffic were of several types and dimensions ranging from the small boat (Bohrnachen), which was 6-8 feet wide, 42-48 feet long, and carried a load of up to 15 tons, to the large Rhine barge, which was 12-15 feet wide, 72-80 feet long, and could carry a maximum load of 150 tons. But a large number of these boats were idle, and the conditions of the more than 200 boatmen's families in Trier and Koblenz was critical.[3] Most of the traffic on the Moselle had again become military with the onset of the Napoleonic wars. As a result, the Principle of Free Navigation meant little to the boatmen of the Moselle valley. In an 1806 petition, they complained that almost all their boats, anchors, ropes, and sailing gear had been requisitioned, either for river transport or for the bridges; that navigation on the river had almost totally ceased; and that their tow-horses had been either stolen or killed during the requisitions.

Under these circumstances, the high ideals of the French Revolution could not be effective in restoring the Moselle valley's former trade prosperity. Nor could the many canalization or improvement projects be carried out. But the Principle of Free Navigation was to survive and be enforced from 1815 on, and with it came the possibility of removing the obstacles and reactivating the river trade of once-flourishing cities.

3 F.A. de Gavarelle, *Abhandlung über die Schiffbarmachung der Lahn, Nahe, Mosel, Saar. Ein Betrag zu einer wirklichen Handlungs-Verbesserung* (Koblenz: 1806).

In order to understand the evolution of the idea of free navigation in Europe since the beginning of the nineteenth century, one must be familiar with the major political and legal developments relating to inland navigation during the period 1815-71.

We have seen that by 1797 the French Republic had secured the German Rhine as its northeastern boundary. At the same time, pro-French republican régimes had been established in Holland and Switzerland, which had become known as "Batavian Republic" and "Helvetic Republic" respectively. In 1806, less than two years after becoming Emperor, Napoleon I consolidated French control over western and central Europe, including the Rhine basin, by dissolving the Holy Roman Germanic Empire and establishing the "Confederation of the Rhine," which included all German States except Prussia and Austria, and which became part of the Napoleonic Continental System. Finally, in 1810, Napoleon incorporated the Batavian Republic, the North German States of Münster, Oldenburg, Hanover (part), and the free cities of Bremen, Hamburg, and Lübeck into the French Empire. Thus, the period 1792-1814 was characterized by a gradual takeover and finally a total control of the Rhine basin by the French.

But the treaties of 1814-15 following the downfall of Napoleon I did not restore the status quo ante.

1 The Holy Roman Empire was not revived. Instead, the very loose German Confederation was established in 1815, including all the small and medium-sized German States, the German-speaking parts of Prussia and Austria, Luxembourg, and Holstein. It was, however, a mere alliance of sovereign States with very little federal executive power.[4]

2 Given this loose political arrangement, and an unprecedented period of peace and prosperity which lasted a century and was interrupted by local conflicts only (Austro-Prussian and Franco-Prussian wars, 1866-67 and 1870-71), this period was one "characterized in general by a fairly close economic and political cooperation between European States, large and small. This came to be known as le concert européen,"[5] which provided for cooperation in a number of specific areas, including inland navigation, through a series of agreements both formal and unwritten, and diplomatic conferences, and which was primarily aimed at insuring "the prosperity of the peoples and the preservation of peace in Europe."[6] These aims would be guaranteed by the great powers: England, France, Russia, Prussia, and Austria.

3 Even though this system provided for a minimum of stability, it was based on the concept of the Nation-State as the only viable framework for political

4 Roger Pinto, *Les organisations européennes* (Paris: Payot, 1963), pp. 15-19.
5 See Cermakian, "Europe's Inland Waterways," *California Engineer* **44**, no. 3 (1965): 12.
6 Pinto, *Les organisations européennes*, pp. 10-12.

sovereignty, an idea inherited from the principles of the French Revolution. Therefore, a State, no matter how small, would give up even part of its sovereignty to a federal or supranational authority only reluctantly. This period witnessed the rise of Prussian power and its eventual hegemony over most of the Rhine basin by 1871. Prussia made considerable territorial gains in the Rhineland (1815) and in northern Germany (1867), and took Alsace-Lorraine away from France (1871), thus denying the latter what partial control it had retained until then in the Rhine and Moselle valleys. Prussia also initiated and directed the German Zollverein (customs union) from 1834 on, and became the leading State in the federal German Empire founded in 1871. Thus, within 50 years, French domination had given way to Prussian hegemony over the Rhine basin.

Just as there was a gradual shift in the balance of power and in the resulting control of inland waterways in west-central Europe, there was also a slow evolution in the idea of free navigation between 1792 and 1871. This is evidenced by the long succession of treaties and conventions drafted and ratified by two or more States with respect to navigation on the Rhine and its tributaries between 1803 and 1868.[7]

The first international treaties concerning free navigation were signed in 1803 and 1804 between France and the Holy Roman Empire. The 1803 treaty dealt with the problem of compensations and indemnities to be paid to German princes who had lost their territories west of the Rhine. In addition to some territorial exchanges, these compensations included a share of the navigation octroi, a single duty which was substituted to the numerous tolls in existence until then. Article 39 stipulated that "All the tolls on the Rhine collected either on the right bank or on the left are abolished, with no possibility of reestablishing them under any name, except for customs duties and a navigation octroi."[8]

The octroi was to be collected jointly by France and the Empire, and the total amount to be paid was not to exceed the total amount of the former tolls. Non-German and non-French craft were to be charged higher duties than French or German ones, and upbound craft more than downbound. The proceeds of the octroi were allocated to cover administrative and police expenses, to pay for the maintenance and repair of tow-paths and of the river channel, and to compensate the German princes for lost territory. The French government, the Emperor, and the local rulers were to meet annually and decide in common upon required improvements in navigation within their respective boundaries. No specific

---

7 The most complete edition of these documents is: Zentral-Kommission für die Rheinschiffahrt, *Rheinurkunden* (2 vols; The Hague, Munich, and Leipzig: 1918); this publication contains the most important texts concerning navigation on the Rhine and its tributaries between 1803 and 1918, reprinted in their respective original languages (French, German, or Dutch).

8 *Ibid.,* "Reichs-Deputations-Hauptschluss" (in French) I, p. 4.

mention was made of free navigation or of the legal status applicable to the major tributaries of the Rhine.

In 1804, the octroi treaty between the Holy Roman Emperor and Napoleon I (who had just become Emperor of the French) reaffirmed the validity of the 1803 treaty and restated the basic principle of Rhine navigation: "Although the thalweg of the Rhine is, with respect to sovereignty, the limit between France and Germany, the Rhine will always be considered, in relation to navigation and commerce, as a river common to both empires ... and navigation on it will be subject to common regulations."[9]

The treaty dealt in detail with the administrative structure of the octroi authority, the nature and amount of the duties to be paid, and the rules governing river traffic. The duties were to be paid according to distance travelled, boat capacity, and load carried. Twelve octroi offices were established, 6 on each bank. Former transit and transfer duties at Cologne and Mainz were abolished, but both cities became mandatory break-in-bulk points for traffic in both directions; accordingly, moderate port and warehousing fees had to be paid in both places. Finally, the maintenance of tow-paths was to be carried out by the French and German Imperial governments, whereas levees and flood-control works were to be cared for by local authorities and private property owners along the riverbanks.

A consideration of the 1803 and 1804 treaties indicates that the idea of free navigation was not entirely accepted during this period, because
1 foreign boats were not yet given equal treatment with French or German ones;
2 although the octroi was in theory a duty collected only to help pay for improvements in navigation, part of its proceeds were used to pay off the dispossessed German princes;
3 with the exception of the Main between Mainz and Frankfurt, the provisions of the treaties did not apply to navigation on tributaries of the Rhine.

However, it could be argued that the left-bank tributaries, including the Moselle, lying as they did in French territory, did not need to be subject to international agreements on the matter since the 1792 decree had extended the principle of free navigation to *all* rivers, not just the Rhine; but this did not prevent the French authorities from imposing new navigation duties on Moselle traffic in 1806.

The 1806 treaty establishing the Confederation of the Rhine and dissolving the Holy Roman Empire merely transferred the authority to regulate navigation and collect the octroi on the German bank from the Empire to the Confederation, while reaffirming the principles and statutes embodied in previous treaties.

---

9 *Ibid.,* "Oktroivertrag zwischen dem Deutschen Reich und Frankreich" (in French) I, p. 6.

The expansion of the French Empire in 1810 to include Holland and northern Germany was not followed by the extension to those provinces of the freedom of navigation enjoyed elsewhere on French inland waterways. All former tolls and duties were abolished in both provinces as of 1 January 1812, but the octroi levied on the Franco-German section of the Rhine was extended to the Dutch Rhine, Waal, Lek, Meuse, Ijssel, and Ems rivers. Thirteen octroi offices were established on those rivers, and the regulations concerning navigation on the upper Rhine were extended to *all* waterways in Holland and northern Germany. Even though the octroi rates charged on Dutch and North German waterways were moderate, their very existence gave William I of Orange-Nassau, reinstated as King of the Netherlands at the end of 1813, a good reason to eliminate them as of 1 January 1814, and restore the former tolls, transit duties, and other taxes; these would be collected in a lump sum by a single office close to the German border for the sake of economy and efficiency.

But the Dutch case of a return to the status quo ante was an exception. After Napoleon's downfall, most western and central European states realized that it was in everyone's best interest, "regardless of their geographic location, to facilitate circulation on all major waterways."[10] This awareness brought about a gradual liberalization of navigation on the Rhine between 1814 and 1868.

Article 5 of 1814 Paris peace treaty between France and the Allies thus provided for free navigation on the Rhine "from the point where it becomes navigable to the sea and vice-versa," with no restriction for anyone. The article also stated that the question of duties to be levied by the riparian states was to be dealt with at the Congress of Vienna, hopefully "in the most equitable and favorable way with regard to the commerce of all nations." Nor was the matter of tributary rivers neglected. According to the same article, the Congress of Vienna would have to decide "in which way, in order to facilitate the communications between the peoples and make them less foreign unto one another [free navigation on the Rhine] might also be extended to all the other rivers which, in their navigable stretches, separate or cross various States."[11]

During the sessions of the Congress of Vienna in 1815, a Commission on the Free Navigation of Rivers was formed and met between 2 February and 24 March 1815. Its meetings were organized by the delegates of France, Prussia, England, and Austria, and were also attended by representatives from Holland, Bavaria, Baden, Hessen-Darmstadt, and Nassau. Most of the delegates and representatives submitted draft proposals to the Commission, which took all their suggestions into account and incorporated them into the "regulations concerning free navigation on rivers" on 24 March. These regulations were in turn appended to the Congress of Vienna Closing Act of 9 June 1815.

---

10 Bonét-Maury, *Les Actes,* introduction, p. 6.
11 *Ibid.,* "Traité de Paris du 30 mai 1814," p. 9.

The main body of the Vienna Closing Act laid down the general rules of free navigation in its Articles 108-117. These rules applied in all states "which are separated or crossed by the same navigable river," and were to become applicable within 6 months after the end of the Congress. Navigation on such rivers was to be free under uniform regulations for all users. Duties charged on river traffic were to be established on the basis of uniform criteria. They could vary from place to place but would have to be moderate — in any case not in excess of the Rhine octroi established in 1804 — and could be increased only after unanimous agreement by all riparian states concerned. The number of duty collection offices was to be as small as possible in order to prevent delays in river traffic. No new mandatory transit or transfer duties could be established, and existing ones were to be abolished except where "locally necessary or useful to navigation and commerce in general." Provisions were made for separate navigation and customs duty collection offices, so that the latter would not interfere with the progress of river traffic. Finally, the maintenance of tow-paths and the improvement of river channels were to be the responsibility of the individual riparian states.

These principles were rather vague and open to various interpretations. The regulations concerning navigation on specific rivers were more detailed but still open to debate. Details concerning duties and administration were to be established in a later convention. On the other hand, a Central Rhine Commission was created "in order to establish a precise control of the obedience to the common rules and to form an authority which could act as a means of communication between riparian States with regard to navigation." The exact functions of the Commission would be determined by later conventions.

With regard to the major tributaries of the Rhine (Neckar, Main, Moselle), and other international waterways (Meuse, Scheldt), freedom of navigation was to be effective "from the point at which each river becomes navigable to its mouth." The member states of the Central Rhine Commission who also exercised political control along the banks of the Meuse and Moselle rivers were to draw up a set of regulations for the latter, similar to the rules governing navigation on the Rhine. Maintenance and improvement of the tow-paths and riverbed were also the responsibility of riparian States, as in the case of the Rhine. Freedom of navigation for the citizens of the states bordering the Neckar, Main, and Moselle was guaranteed on the Meuse and Rhine. As for the Scheldt, the rules concerning navigation were to be set later "in the most favorable manner for trade and navigation, and as similarly as possible to what has been set for the Rhine."[12]

Although these principles were universally accepted, they were also interpreted very differently by every State concerned. The Dutch, who had

12 *Ibid.*, "Congrès de Vienne: Annexe 16B du 24 mars 1815," p. 10.

re-established tolls on their waterways in 1814, gave a very narrow interpretation to the idea of the point where the Rhine reached the sea. They contended that the sea began where the influence of the tides could still be felt, so that the mouths of the Rhine, according to this definition, were some 90 km distant from the sea; thus, tolls could be collected along most of the Dutch Rhine.[13] Moreover, the Dutch argued that "only the Lek was to be considered as the continuation of (the Rhine) in the Netherlands," whereas the rulers of Prussia, Bavaria, Hessen, Baden, and France contended that free navigation rights applied to "all the distributaries and mouths of (the Rhine) in the Netherlands, without any distinction."[14] This so-called "quarrel of the rivermouths" was finally settled in 1831, when the Mainz convention established the rules for navigation on the Rhine, including both the Lek and Waal in Holland. The Mainz convention also provided for collection of navigation duties, which would be strictly enforced and whose proceeds would be used only for the maintenance of the river channel. No mention was made of rules concerning the Rhine tributaries, but duty-free ports were to be provided on the Moselle, Main, and Neckar, as they had been on the Rhine, for the purpose of free storage of goods to be transshipped.

The Mannheim convention of 1868 was the final step in the evolution towards completely free navigation during this period, although the Versailles Treaty of 1919 was the one which really completed the evolution, as will be seen later. At Mannheim, free navigation on the Rhine was proclaimed "from Basle to the open sea," rather than "from the point where it becomes navigable to its mouth." This was a definite extension of the privilege, and was part of the financial settlement of the rivermouth problem.[15] Since the latter essentially hinged upon a matter of tolls, the other part of the settlement was spelled out in Article 3 which abolished tolls altogether: "No duty based solely on navigation shall be collected on craft or freight, nor on [timber] rafts sailing on the Rhine or its tributaries, provided that [the latter] be located in the territory of the High Contracting Parties."[16]

These provisions also applied to all other waterways in Holland and to those between Holland and Belgium, provided the craft belonged to citizens of one of the Rhine's riparian states. In addition to this restriction, the closing protocol stated that exemption from tolls did not apply for the operation of

---

13 Pierre Michelet, *Les transports au sol et l'organisation de l'Europe* (Paris: Payot, 1962), p. 22.

14 Rheinschiffahrtskarte (German/French) in *Rheinurkunden* (Mainz, 1831) I, p. 213.

15 The question of free navigation on the Scheldt and on the international waterways common to Belgium and the Netherlands (known as les eaux intermédiaires) had already been settled in the London Treaty of 1839 establishing the independence of Belgium.

16 "Convention révisée, pour la navigation du Rhin, signée à Mannheim le 17 octobre 1868 ...," Bonét-Maury, *Les Actes*, p. 11.

draw-bridges, the utilization of artificial waterways, or the building, maintenance, and operation of locks. This provision would later allow the Germans to improve and canalize the Main and Neckar and charge tolls on both rivers. It was also the basis for the more recent decision to charge tolls on the canalized Moselle between Thionville and Koblenz.

Finally, the basic statutes of the Central Rhine Commission were set forth in Article 44 of the Mannheim convention. These statutes, as amended in 1919 and 1945, still govern the Commission today. It is only an advisory body, with very limited executive powers, and can hardly be said to control navigation on the Rhine. Its advice is highly respected by member States, however, and its contribution to international river transport has been great. The chief problem is that its competence was never extended to the tributaries of the Rhine, which continued to be administered, maintained, and improved by national or regional public works authorities, with little or no international cooperation.

MOSELLE IMPROVEMENT PROJECTS DURING THE 19TH CENTURY

France

Once more, in 1815, the political and economic circumstances had changed. Monarchy was restored in France. For the first time, France and Prussia had a common boundary, since Prussia had replaced the Elector of Trier as the governing power in the German Moselle valley; and Luxembourg lost the right bank of the Moselle between Apach and Trier to Prussia. But despite territorial changes, projects to improve the navigability of the Moselle were initiated in all three states with due regard to previous studies and projects, under the impetus of engineers, administrators, industrial managers, and politicians.

The first pressure group to act in this direction was the Chamber of Commerce of Metz, founded by decree in 1815, which took up the question of navigation on the Moselle from the very start. However, the urgency to take some action became apparent only in 1825, when the Dutch decided to establish a steamboat service on the Rhine up to Strasbourg. This project would have suppressed what little traffic there was on the Moselle. In view of this threat, the Chamber petitioned the government to reassess the physical obstacles to navigation described in the Gardeur-Lebrun report of 1772 in order to determine what improvements were to be made, and "to agree with the Prussian Government, so that the latter act on its part in those sections which require, on its territory, the same measures, which will be easy to carry out through a joint Commission made up of [representatives of] the Governments concerned."[17]

17 Albert Houpert, *La Moselle navigable* (Metz: Chambre de Commerce de Metz, 1932), p. 25.

But the Chamber unanimously decided that improvements would have to be carried out in the French sector first, before bargaining with Prussia. A commission would be responsible for the execution of the necessary work on the Moselle as far south as Pagny; from there, a link could easily be established with the Meuse and the Ardennes Canal, presumably through a more northerly route than the Moselle-Meuse link proposed by Vauban in 1658. At this time, the government was undertaking the survey of a route for the Marne-Rhine Canal, and in 1827, a Royal Ordinance authorized the study of a Moselle-Saône link based on the findings of Lecreulx. But very little came of these investigations. In 1833 the Minister of the Interior granted the meager amount of 40,000 francs "for the dredging of the river and the removal of stones and rocks," and in the same year, two civil engineers, Le Masson and Le Joindre, sailed down the Moselle between La Lobe (20 km south of Metz) and Koblenz to study the physical obstacles in the riverbed and to recommend means of removing them. Their recommendations, along with further pressure by the Chamber on the government, led to the passing of the law of 1835 "concerning the improvement of navigation on rivers," which provided a subsidy of 6 million francs for this purpose, 1 million of which was to be granted for the improvement of the Moselle between Frouard and the Prussian border.

In their 1833 report, Le Masson and Le Joindre stated that the main obstacles to navigation on the Moselle were the gravel banks or shallows (hauts-fonds) which separated the much longer stretches of deep water. Over a distance of some 80 km between La Lobe and the Prussian border, there were 40 such shallows, or one every 2 km, the average length of each shallow being 220 m, or one-ninth of the total length considered. The suggested solution was to work on the shallows, not by eliminating them completely, but by narrowing the river channel through the construction of longitudinal levees in those sections. The levees would be connected with the riverbank upstream from the shallows, and would be submerged during periods of high water. They would help raise the stream level and increase stream velocity, and this in turn would cut down the shallows, thus allowing for a minimum depth of 1 m during the summertime low-water mark and 1.4m during the remaining 8 months. The project was successfully carried out between 1837 and 1842 according to these principles.[18]

During the 1840's, the construction of the Marne-Rhine Canal resulted in a new campaign by the Metz Chamber of Commerce to build a lateral canal along the Moselle between Metz and Frouard, where the Rhine-Marne Canal intersects the Moselle. The longitudinal levee method used previously was rejected because it could not provide the same draft as the Marne-Rhine Canal, i.e., a minimum

---

18 Le Masson and Le Joindre, *Notice sur le système et les résultats des travaux adoptés pour l'amélioration de la navigation de la Moselle* (Metz: 1838).

depth of 1.80 m. After numerous studies and proposals, and an unrelenting campaign lasting 25 years, the government finally granted the authorization to build a lateral canal along the Moselle between Frouard and Thionville. The main objection had been financial. It was removed when local authorities and the metal-working industry agreed to provide the necessary funds (some 11.5 million francs). The Imperial Decree[19] of 1867, and the law passed during the same year, provided for "the execution of the works planned to improve navigation on the Moselle between Frouard and Thionville."

Between Frouard and Metz, the project included improvement of the riverbed over a distance of 38 km and the construction of 6 lateral canals totalling 10.5 km, with a minimum depth of 2 m. The difference in elevation to be overcome was 22.3m; this was to be accomplished by means of 9 locks, 40 m long, 6 m wide, and at least 2 m deep. The problem of the shallows was to be overcome by the construction of 7 dams across the river in critical locations; this provided a minimum depth of 2.25m in the riverbed. Two branch canals were also to be added to the main waterway, totalling 5.3 km. One was to serve the ironworks at Ars-sur-Moselle, the other one the railroad station in Metz. Finally, 12 ports were to be built along the waterway, including those serving the metal-working plants at Pont-à-Mousson and Novéant.[20]

By the time the Franco-Prussian war began in July 1870, the problem of canalizing the Moselle through Metz had not yet been solved, since the civil engineers' plans were at odds with the military authorities' requirements. Nor had the improvement of the Metz-Thionville section been planned in detail. Finally, in the Frouard-Metz section, some 20 km between Arnaville and Metz remained to be improved according to the 1867 specifications, although this part of the river had already been improved somewhat by the longitudinal levees method in 1842.

Prussia and Luxembourg

Thus, the campaign of the Metz Chamber of Commerce to improve navigation on the Moselle had yielded some results in the French sector by 1870. It had also had its repercussions in Prussia. In 1828, a report concerning navigation on the Moselle was written for the Prussian government, and in 1833, the Provincial Assembly of the Rhineland sent a petition to King Frederick William III

---

19 France was a kingdom from 1815 to 1848, a republic from 1848 to 1851, an empire (ruled by Napoleon III) from 1851 to 1871, and a republic since (except for the period 1940-44, when it was governed by the pro-German régime of Marshal Philippe Pétain).

20 Henri-Félix Frécot, "Navigation sur la Moselle: amélioration entre Frouard et Thionville, rapport de l'Ingénieur en Chef" (1870) in *Berichte der französischen Präfekten und Oberingenieure über den Stand der Wasserbau-Verwaltung in Elsass-Lothringen für das Jahr 1870* (Strasbourg: 1873), p. 79.

requesting improvement of navigation conditions on the river. Accordingly, the Prussian government undertook dredging operations in the riverbed between Trier and Koblenz from 1836 to 1857, so as to guarantee a minimum depth for river traffic. In 1825, the Prussians had also started negotiations with Luxembourg resulting in joint dredging operations on the Moselle between Trier and the Franco-Prussian border.[21]

Under the rule of William I, King of the Netherlands, Luxembourg sought to revive once again the old project of the Moselle-Meuse link through the Ardennes. The early project was to have followed the Ourthe, Clerf, Wiltz, Sûre, and Alzette rivers to Luxembourg, and from there the route of the Old Mansfeld project to the Moselle. Because of strategic considerations, later plans had the main route follow the Sûre River to its confluence with the Moselle at Wasserbillig, with a southward branch to Luxembourg. The canal was to have included 150 locks and allowed navigation of 40-ton barges. The project was begun in 1828 but interrupted in 1831 following the independence of Belgium. In the mid-nineteenth century, a Belgian engineer would have used the same route (Alzette and Sûre) as part of the grandiose North Sea-to-Black Sea "Central Axis of European Inland Navigation" scheme, which never materialized; it would have required a far greater degree of cooperation than the European States were ready to engage in during this period. For (with the exception of the Rhine) waterways, like other means of transport, served the economic and political interests of national governments and reinforced their tendencies towards centralization.

TRAFFIC ON THE MOSELLE RIVER BETWEEN 1815 AND 1871

The political and technical obstacles to navigation on the Moselle did not prevent a rebirth of some commercial activity on the river after 1815. The major reason was the abolition of former tolls and other duties from 1792 on, except for those in Luxembourg, the latter being under the authority of the Dutch who did not intend to give up their right of collecting tolls. But a Dutch Royal Decree of 1819 did abolish all duties on the Moselle. Reinstated in 1822 to help pay for the maintenance of tow-paths, tolls were abolished for good in Luxembourg in 1862. In France, even though there were no tolls on the waterways, a system of indirect taxes had been imposed on boatmen in 1793 (on the Moselle in 1806); these taxes were reduced in 1839 and eliminated only as late as 1880 to help inland water transport compete with the then flourishing railroad companies.[22]

21 Chambre de Commerce de Metz, *La Chambre de Commerce de Metz: 1815-1922* (Metz: 1922), p. 17.
22 Dominique Renouard, *Les transports de marchandises par fer, route et eau depuis 1850* (Paris: Fondation Nationale des Sciences Politiques, 1960), p. 59.

The other major reason for the rebirth of commercial river traffic on the Moselle was technological. Rowing-boats and horse-drawn barges were increasingly replaced by steam-powered craft on the Rhine after 1825. On the Moselle, steam navigation began in 1839 with the trial run of the steamboat "Ville de Metz" between Metz and Trier. Regularly scheduled steamboat services were established soon thereafter between the two cities and extended to Koblenz in 1841. Three steamboats were used, with a power of 30 hp and a capacity of 60 passengers each. In 1845, they transported an estimated 47,000 passengers and 3835 tons of freight. There were two round trips per week between Metz and Koblenz. The Metz company operating this service was dissolved in 1851, and it was taken over by a new company founded in Trier during the same year. This company ran three 60-hp boats and stayed in operation until 1870. It carried some 41,000 passengers and 11,153 tons of freight in 1866.[23]

But steamboats were by no means the only craft used in those days. As early as 1805, Pierre Chedeaux, who was to become the first President of the Metz Chamber of Commerce, had already organized regular river transport down the Moselle as far as Trier, Koblenz, Cologne, Düsseldorf, Frankfurt, and Mainz. In 1816, there was considerable freight traffic between Metz and Trier, although the nature and volume of the goods carried are nowhere mentioned. Most of this traffic took place in a variety of barges ranging from the rowing-boat (2 m wide and 13 m long) to the "large boat," (3.5 m wide and 22 m long) which could carry loads of 220 tons downbound and 120 tons upbound, and had to be towed by no less than 6 horses.

The most detailed description of traffic on the Moselle during this period is found in the Le Masson-Le Joindre report. Not only did the authors survey the physical obstacles to navigation, but they also analyzed the traffic patterns during the 1823-33 decade, based on data provided by the Administration of Indirect Taxes (which was responsible for collecting the navigation duties on the Moselle since 1806). The 1833 figures will appear to be minimal, but it must be remembered that this was before the Industrial Revolution transformed the economy of Lorraine, and that physical conditions for navigation were far from satisfactory; it was also a few years before steamboats began to operate. Four kinds of barges were used, with the following lengths and carrying capacities:

23 Otto Beck, *Beschreibung des Regierungsbezirks Trier* (Trier: 1871), p. 35. "In 1830, the first regularly scheduled boat line for passenger transport was established between Trier and Koblenz and later extended to Metz. There then was one steamboat a day in each direction" (Pierre Hamer, "Esquisse d'une histoire des voies de communication au Grand-Duché de Luxembourg" in *La Moselle: son passé, son avenir*, p. 41). However, none of the other sources refer to this service, and give 1839 as the starting date for the Metz company.

Type of boat	Length	Carrying capacity
Grand bateau (Grossschiff)	34 m	200 tons
Bateau-loge (Traubert)	26 m	85 tons
Caine (Kaine)	12 m	75 tons
Champ de vigne (Bohrnachen)	10 m	30 tons

There was a great variety in the main types of freight carried. The down-bound traffic was made up of the following:

a construction timber from the Vosges floated down the Meurthe and Moselle to sawmills in Metz, Belgium, the German Moselle valley, and the Rhineland;

b firewood in logs carried by boats;

c goods from southern France transshipped in Metz and bound for Trier, Koblenz, and Cologne: madder from Avignon, olive oil, thistle from Provence, brandy, fine wines, bronze ornaments, and time-pieces;

d furniture manufactured in Metz, which had become the chief export from that city to Trier; before 1815, the major item had been wine grown in the Metz area, but its export had dwindled thereafter due to excessive Prussian customs duties;

e iron ore from Hayange shipped down to ironworks located in the Moselle valley downstream from Trier.

The upbound traffic was made up of the following:

a goods shipped to Metz from Cologne, Koblenz, and Trier: pipe clay (also known as Cologne clay), hardware goods, pig-iron, copper, lead, lead ore, iron and brass wire, steel ingots, slate, sandstone pottery, mineral waters, and grain (when the import of the latter was permitted);

b coal from the Saarbrücken coalfields, shipped down the Saar River to Konz (at the Saar-Moselle confluence) and up the Moselle to Sierck, Thionville, Uckange, Metz, and Pont-à-Mousson, for use in local ironworks;

c cobblestones from the Sierck quarries;

d plaster from Koenigsmacker;

e firewood.

Most of the goods originating in or bound for the Rhine valley had to be transshipped at Koblenz since Moselle craft seldom travelled on the Rhine itself (only occasionally did they venture as far as Cologne). This was probably the result of a near-monopoly of traffic held by Dutch and German barge and steamboat operators on the Rhine during this period.

The report gave approximate figures for both downbound and upbound traffic on the Moselle downstream of Metz in 1833, as follows (in metric tons):

Downbound		Upbound	
Iron ore	700	Coal	27,000
Grain and scrap	100	Grain	2,200
Other items	1,200	Plaster and cobblestones	300
		Slate	200
		Other items	1,300
	2,000		31,000

Thus, there was a very serious imbalance between downbound and upbound traffic, for no return freight could match the bulky shipments of coal and grain. If those two items had been removed, traffic in both directions would have been reduced to a trickle. The authors' contention that the Moselle between Koblenz and Metz carried about one-third of the volume transported on the Canal du Midi, and two-thirds of the freight carried by the St Etienne-Andrézieux railroad of east-central France has little meaning in this context, for France was still in the pre-heavy industry age, and the impact of large-scale railroad construction would not be felt for another 25 years. The goods carried on the Moselle in 1833 were still mostly those which had made up the bulk of the river's trade in the seventeenth and eighteenth centuries, although the beginnings of an important coal and iron ore traffic were already developing.

The turning point in the industrialization of Lorraine came in the late 1840s, when the ironworks, which until then had used mostly charcoal derived from local forest resources, turned increasingly to the use of coke imported from outside the area, mostly from the Saar. This change resulted in the construction of a great number of new ironworks in and around the Moselle valley, and the expansion and modernization of the older ones. By 1870, most of the plants were using coke, but they were still small in size, and being dependent upon low-grade, phosphorous iron ore (known as minette), produced a rather poor-quality pig-iron, unfit for the steel produced by the Bessemer process. Only after the introduction of the Gilchrist-Thomas process in 1880 did Lorraine iron works change over to large-scale steel production.

Thus, if it is true that the Industrial Revolution of the nineteenth century was primarily a steel revolution, the Lorraine ironworks were not affected by it until very late. Their average size remained small, and their traffic in raw materials as well as finished products was never large enough to warrant any spectacular river improvement projects. In Frécot's progress report of the Frouard-Metz waterway in 1870, traffic statistics for the Frouard to Pont-à-Mousson section in May and June of that year reflect both the importance of the ironworks industry to the local economy in that it accounted for a large share of the total traffic, and the relatively small size of the plants reflected in the small volumes of goods carried:

Downbound traffic		Upbound traffic	
Coal	1,764	Pig-iron	1,423
Coke	3,023	Beech wood	133
Pig-iron	17		
Sand	352		
Fir timber	1,236		
	6,392 tons		1,556 tons

The relative stagnation of the iron industry during this period was due also to the development of the railroad network. The Nancy-Metz line was opened in 1850, the Metz-Saarbrücken line in 1851, the Paris-Nancy-Strasbourg line in 1852, and the Metz-Thionville line in 1854. There is no doubt that the development of the railroad network in Lorraine was partly related to the growth of the iron industry: in 1854, the Nancy-Metz line had a freight traffic of some 223,000 tons, far in excess of Moselle river traffic in 1870.[24] However, the construction of the French railroad network before 1870 reflects strategic as well as economic motives, i.e., the desire of the central government to control its border provinces as firmly as possible. It was in the nation's best interest to have fast communications with those provinces, and unwise to foster large-scale industrial developments so close to the border. Accordingly, the Moselle (a slow means of transport and primarily an industrial route serving a border province) was at a great political disadvantage with respect to the railroads.

24 "Carte figurative du trafic marchandises des chemins de fer français: 1854" in Renouard, *Les transports de marchandises*, separate map.

IV

Franco-German Rivalry in the Moselle Valley (1871-1945)

As a result of its defeat during the Franco-Prussian war in 1871, France lost Alsace and the northern half of Lorraine for nearly 50 years. The new border bisected the Moselle valley near Pagny, some 20 km south of Metz, leaving that French-speaking city in German territory. According to Hartshorne,[1] the demarcation of the border was based primarily on cultural and strategic, rather than economic, factors. Metz was a key fortress essential for the defense of the border; and most of the annexed territory was German-speaking. Hartshorne contended that the Germans' desire to control the Lorraine iron ore deposits was not the dominant factor, because the ore was unfit for steelmaking at that time. Nevertheless, "the boundary change of 1871 brought the greater part of the Lorraine iron industry, with the Saar coalfield, within the limits of the German Reich," and the new boundary "had an important influence on the growth of the [Lorraine] iron and steel industry" (see Figure 3).[2] The inclusion of large iron ore and coal deposits close to each other and within the same customs union had the net result of an intensified exchange of ore and coal, and therefore led to improvements in the transportation network. Although the railroad was the chief beneficiary of these improvements, the campaign to canalize the

1 Richard Hartshorne, "The Franco-German Boundary of 1871," *World Politics* II (1950): 209-50.
2 Norman J.G. Pounds and William N. Parker, *Coal and Steel in Western Europe* (Bloomington: Indiana University Press, 1957), p. 183.

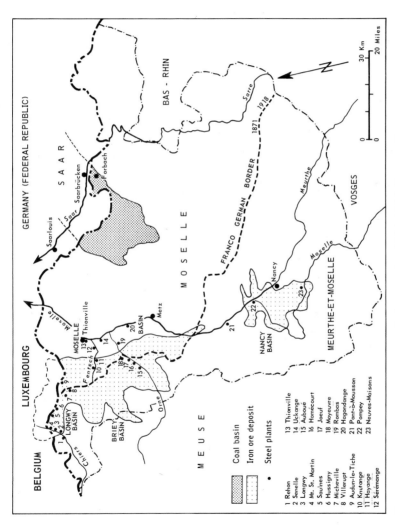

Figure 3 The Moselle River in relation to the 1871-1918 Franco-German border in Alsace-Lorraine, showing the localization of the present iron and steel plants, coalfields, and iron ore deposits.

55

Moselle became more active than ever in view of the advantages heavy industry could be expected to derive from inland water transport.

Industrialization of Lorraine

With the establishment of the 1871 border, Germany acquired 25 blast-furnaces with an output of 204,579 metric tons (1867) and 13 iron-ore concessions with a total area of 9031 hectares. This amounted to "nearly 80 per cent of the conceded area of the ore-field and a similar proportion of its productive capacity."[3] France was left only with the deposits and ironworks of the Longwy (near Luxembourg) and Nancy areas. The net result of this situation in the part of Lorraine which remained French was to speed up the development of the iron industry in order to compensate for the loss of productive capacity to Germany. This effort was largely successful since, with more limited resources, French Lorraine soon exceeded the pre-war production of the whole province: by 1900 it was "producing about 60 per cent of France's pig-iron," thanks partly to the discovery and exploitation of the Briey iron ore deposits in the 1880s and 1890s.[4] On the other hand, few ironworks were founded during those two decades on the French side of the border: five ironworks in the Nancy area (of which two were the result of the new border), three in the Longwy area, and one steel plant built by De Wendel at Joeuf right across the border from its ironworks at Hayange. This relatively slow initial development was largely due to political, technological, and economic factors.

Political: According to the so-called politique du glacis (glacis policy), the French government deliberately discouraged the establishment of finished-product metalworking industries in areas close to the border, thereby restricting the local market of the ironworks. At the same time, restrictions were placed upon the acquisition of new iron ore concessions in the Nancy area, in which front-line fortifications had been built after the defeat of 1871 to replace those around Metz; this restricted the raw materials base of ironworks in and around Nancy.

Technological: Under the Bessemer steel process, the pig-iron had to be phosphorus-free. The Lorraine pig-iron, made of local iron ore, had a very high phosphorus content. It was therefore unfit for steel-making and production of pig-iron would therefore have little reason to increase.

Economic: During the 1870s and 1880s, the prevailing philosophy was to develop the already established ironworks in northern and central France while

3 *Ibid.*, p. 195; and Anon., "Influence de la cession de l'Alsace-Lorraine à l'Allemagne sur l'industrie métallurgique," *Revue Universelle des Mines* (Liège) XXIX (1871): 241-50.
4 E. Gréau, *Le fer en Lorraine* (Nancy: 1908), pp. 35-8; Ch. Palgen, *Les nouveaux sondages du bassin minier entre Moselle et Meuse* (Extrait des Mémoires de l'Union des Ingénieurs de Louvain, Louvain: 1900), 22 pp.; and Pounds and Parker, *Coal and Steel*, p. 196.

disregarding the economic potentials of the northeast. Most of the capital lay in the hands of northern and central corporations, who were reluctant to invest in an area of potentially serious competition. Whenever outside capital was invested in Lorraine ironworks, it was with the idea of exporting pig-iron to other regions for fabrication. Much of the capital invested during this period was native to the Longwy, Nancy, and Metz areas. In the latter case, the De Wendel family, who had owned ironworks in the Moselle valley since 1704, decided to remain there after the German annexation, but found it also profitable to build new plants on the French side of the border, thus benefiting from both markets.

In German Lorraine, ironworks were concentrated mainly along the Moselle and its tributaries, the Orne and Fentsch rivers, with isolated plants at Ottange (near Luxembourg) and Stiring-Wendel (near the Saar border). The latter had been established by the De Wendel family in 1854 along the Metz-Forbach-Saarbrücken railroad. The plant was supplied with nearby Saar coking coal and received Moselle iron ore by rail. With German annexation, preferential railroad freight rates for iron ore were discontinued for the Stiring plant, which had to close down. For the ironworks industry of this area in general, "much of this period was one of economic stringency, when falling prices offered little induce-ment to expansion or experiment."[5] In fact, the industries of German Lorraine were now deprived of their traditional French markets and had to compete with ironworks in other areas of the Zollverein, the Saar and the Ruhr, more powerful and endowed with large local markets. Finally, strategic and technological fac-tors similar to those found in French Lorraine also played an important rôle. As a result, "out of 12 plants with 32 blast-furnaces in 1873, and a pig-iron produc-tion of 274,000 tons, there remained only 7 plants with 17 blast-furnaces and a production of 242,000 tons in 1878."[6] However, despite this decline in pig-iron production, there seems to have been an active coal and iron ore barge traffic on the Moselle and Saar rivers, the Marne-Rhine Canal, and the Saar Coal Mines Canal (built in 1866 parallel to the Saar River between Saarbrücken and the Marne-Rhine Canal); according to Pounds, "Thionville and Metz grew to be important river ports."[7]

What saved the Lorraine iron industry and made for the launching and expan-sion of steel production was the Gilchrist-Thomas basic steel-making process, which allowed phosphorous pig-iron to be used. But there again, the develop-ment of steel-producing capacity was slow. In 1880, exclusive rights to the Thomas patent had been acquired by De Wendel for its plants at Joeuf and

5 Norman J.G. Pounds, "Lorraine and the Ruhr," *Economic Geography* 33, no. 2 (1957): 153.
6 Jean Degott, *La canalisation de la Moselle dans l'économie du charbon et de l'acier* (Metz: Compagnie lorraine d'études et d'expansion, 1961), p. 50.
7 Pounds, "Lorraine and the Ruhr", p. 153.

Hayange and by the Longwy Corporation for its plant at Mont-Saint-Martin. Since the patent did not expire until 1893, it took almost 15 years to establish new steel mills in Lorraine. At the same time, the Ruhr industrialists, who had theretofore ignored the Lorraine iron ore deposits and ironworks, began to gain interest in the now usable iron ore. They started to import large volumes of ore for their ironworks, either by rail (the Thionville-Koblenz line had been completed in 1879), by the Moselle and Rhine rivers, or via the Marne-Rhine Canal, Strasbourg, and the Rhine. Cheaper transport of iron ore through a canalized Moselle was first advocated by the Ruhr steelmakers in the early 1880s. At that time, Lorraine industrialists turned against the project for fear of being denied the resources to expand their own iron and steel production. In fact, it is estimated that Lorraine never shipped more than 20 per cent of its ore to the Ruhr ironworks, whereas it received at least half of its total coal requirements from the Ruhr coal basin by 1890. According to Pounds "the direct interchange of coal and ore between the Ruhr and Lorraine never achieved a greater importance than it possessed in the late '80s and early '90s of the last century."[8] And the interchange seemed to work to the advantage of the Lorraine steel industry.

After a decade of stagnation (1871-80) and a period of slow expansion (1881-95), the Lorraine iron and steel industry experienced a period of unprecedented growth (1895-1913). The main factor in this growth was technical integration, i.e., the concentration of the whole steel-making process into a single operation, from iron ore to rolled-steel products, by grouping together blast-furnace, steel mill, and rolling mill at or near the source of iron ore or coking coal. This integration in turn was made possible by advancements in transportation, "for the saving realized on account of it had to be at least equal to the additional cost involved in the movement of larger volumes of raw materials instead of semi-finished products."[9]

In 1893 and 1901, the German railroads put into effect preferential rates for bulky raw materials, including iron ore and coal, thereby helping the technical integration process. The latter was introduced in the Ruhr in the early 1890s, and German Lorraine followed suit soon after: from 1897 to 1901, 3 steel plants were built in the area, and a fourth one in 1912. The iron and steel industry of French Lorraine followed a similar trend: 8 steel mills were built there between 1895 and 1913 (3 around Nancy, 1 in the Orne valley near the border, and 4 in the Longwy area). However, the French plants concentrated on pig-iron and crude-steel production, so that their integration was not as complete as in the German plants. They were often only branches of corporations based in northern and central France or in Belgium, whose primary aim was to import Lorraine

8 *Ibid.*, p. 154.
9 Degott, *La canalisation de la Moselle*, p. 53.

pig-iron and crude steel to be transformed into rolled-steel products in the mother plants.

Another factor explaining the expansion of the iron and steel industry in Lorraine was the raw materials situation. It seems that most of the German firms owning blast furnaces and steel works in Lorraine had also acquired coal mines in the Ruhr, or had at least contracted agreements or partnerships with Ruhr coal-mining concerns. By 1910, German Lorraine was entirely dependent upon Ruhr coking coal, and shipments from the Saar had been reduced to a trickle. On the other hand, the Ruhr had lessened its dependence upon Lorraine iron ore by importing more and more high-grade ore from Sweden after 1900. By 1910, most of the iron ore mined in German Lorraine was smelted locally, with large shipments to the Saar and lesser ones to the Ruhr. In French Lorraine, a large proportion of the ore was exported to Belgium, and a small amount to German Lorraine, but again most of it was smelted locally. The French plants had more difficulty in securing their coal. They had to import about half of their coke requirements, and about half of those imports came from the Ruhr, although the German Coal Syndicate was reluctant to supply French industry with Ruhr coal and seemed to favor its own nationals. However, Ruhr coal was the best for steel-making, and coal shipments from northern France and Belgium could hardly satisfy the growing demand of French Lorraine steel plants.

Finally, the expansion of the Lorraine iron and steel industry is partly the result of large outside investments after 1900. The case of French Lorraine has been dealt with in connection with the technical integration process. In German Lorraine, Ruhr capital came to dominate the majority of existing companies, and after 1910 began to establish branch plants of Ruhr iron and steel concerns. In 1900, four groups controlled the ownership of steel plants in German Lorraine: the De Wendel family; a group of three Saar corporations; Spaeter, a German industrialist from Koblenz; and six Belgian corporations. The latter two groups fell first under the control of the Ruhr industrialists, who were interested in owning not only pig-iron plants, but fully integrated iron and steel operations. The invasion of Lorraine by Ruhr interests was due partly to the availability of excess capital in the Ruhr, and partly to the overt help of the German government, whose glacis policy did not favor foreign ownership of heavy industry along a strategic border. The government's railroad rate policy and attitude towards canalization of the Moselle also conformed to the interests of the Ruhr industries as opposed to those of Lorraine, Luxembourg, and the Saar.

In 1911, the Ruhr industrialists began building their own branch plants in German Lorraine, with the construction of the giant Thyssen complex at Hagondange. Krupp also bought land at Woippy, near Metz, and Gutehoffnungshütte at Manom, near Thionville, in order to build plants. But their plans were interrupted by the advent of the First World War. Even so, by 1914, the influence of Ruhr industrialists had become predominant in the Lorraine iron and steel industry. Out of an average daily pig-iron production of 11,000 tons, some 5900 tons were produced by Ruhr-owned plants, 1890 by Saar-owned plants, 1795 by Lorraine-owned (De Wendel) plants, and 1415 tons by the independent Rombas plant.[10] With such a large share in the ownership of the area's productive capacity and the building of branch factories there, the Ruhr industrialists began to take the Lorraine's industrial and market problems at heart, and would probably have ceased their opposition to the canalization of the Moselle (and even favored it) if the war had not halted their expansion.

The effects of the First World War were limited in German Lorraine, which was never invaded by Allied troops. Iron and steel production did decline somewhat because of labor shortages, difficulties in obtaining supplies of Ruhr coke (the Germans then regretted not having inland waterway connections between the Ruhr and Lorraine), the shutdown of two plants and the sequestration of enemy-owned plants at Knutange (partly Belgian-owned), Moyeuvre and Hayange (owned by De Wendel, even though this was legally a German corporation and its owners German citizens since 1871). On the other hand, the Germans, after occupying French Lorraine, decided to dismantle the steel plants there, carrying away the most modern equipment and destroying the remainder. They shut down nearly all the pig-iron plants without dismantling them and were ready to reactivate them in case of need. Pig-iron production in French Lorraine fell from 3.5 million tons in 1913 to 15,000 tons in 1915, and was still under 200,000 tons in 1918. In case of victory, the Germans would have annexed all of Lorraine, as stated in a 1917 memorandum addressed to the German government from the steelmakers, in which they argued that long-range foresight made the displacement of the Lorraine border unavoidable and indispensable, for they could not afford to give up French Lorraine's iron ore, and that Germany should not have to depend upon foreign ore supplies. Although this statement clearly indicated the Germans' desire to control their total raw materials requirements, it also came at a time when the Swedish government had imposed statutory limits on the volume of iron ore exports. Such action by a foreign power in wartime — when there was a pressing need to increase steel production for military purposes — had to be avoided in the future. But there is no evidence that this situation led to an increased consumption of Lorraine iron ore in the rest of Germany. The main difficulty was still cheap transportation.

10 Hermann Schumacher, *Die westdeutsche Eisenindustrie und die Moselkanalisierung* (Leipzig: 1910), pp. 24-5; Max Schlenker, *Das Eisenhüttenwesen in Elsass-Lothringen* (Frankfurt: 1919), pp. 197-202 and 225; and Henry Laufenburger, *L'industrie sidérurgique de la Lorraine désannexée et la France* (Strasbourg: 1924), p. 111.

The Railroad Revolution

While the railroad networks of the larger European states were essentially completed by 1870, there were great differences in mileage between the various national networks. But the mileage gap between France and Germany had narrowed considerably since 1850. By then, Germany had completed all of its trunk lines except the Rhine valley line between Bonn and Mainz (completed only in 1858) and including the Mannheim-Saarbrücken line (1847). With 6000 km of track, Germany had built its railroads faster than any other country except Belgium, even though this had been done independently by each state in a piecemeal fashion. France had a far less complete network and only half of Germany's length of track. By 1870, the French Empire had a complete network centered on Paris, with a total length of 17,500 km, on account of Napoleon III's dynamic transport policy. At the same time, Germany had slowly increased its total length of track to 19,500 km, for lack of an overall transport policy. During the following 20 years, both countries more than doubled their respective railroad mileages. This can be explained by the growing industrialization and by the pro-railroad policies of Bismarck in Germany and Freycinet in France.[11] In the latter case, the idea was to build as many local lines and stations as possible "in order to grant all Frenchmen the benefits of proximity to the railroad." This new dual function of the French railroads — as a long-distance bulk carrier and as a local means of transport for small-volume goods — accounts for their increasing share of total traffic in terms of ton-kilometers: from 11 per cent in 1851 to 63 per cent in 1876 and 72 per cent in 1913, while the share of inland waterways dropped from 37 to 15 per cent and rose again to 18 per cent, and while the share of road traffic decreased from 52 to 22 to 10 per cent during the same years. The growth of rail traffic in northeastern France was even greater than the national average: between 1903 and 1913, the volume of goods shipped by rail increased 61 per cent for France as a whole and 128 per cent in the northeast; for water transport, the respective growth rates were 27.5 and 31 per cent. The higher rates for the northeast could be attributed to the enormous expansion of the Lorraine iron and steel industry between 1900 and 1914.

Although the early development of railroads in Lorraine had been related to the growth of the ironworks industry, all major additions which followed were built prior to the great expansion of the steel industry in the 1890s. The Thionville-Longwy-Mézières-Paris line, completed in 1863, was built in order to provide fast communications between Paris and the border regions, and to reinforce

---

11 J.H. Clapham, *The Economic Development of France and Germany, 1815-1914* (4th ed.; Cambridge: Cambridge University Press, 1936, reprinted 1963), pp. 339-40; and W.O. Henderson, *The Industrial Revolution on the Continent: Germany, France, Russia, 1800-1914* (London: 1961), pp. 19-20.

the central government's authority there. The Thionville-Koblenz railroad along the Moselle valley, in the planning stage since 1860, was completed by the Prussian government in 1879 for strategic rather than economic considerations, since the Lorraine iron industry had little or no trade with the Ruhr at that time, and hardly any iron ore was shipped to the Ruhr until a few years later. The Thionville-Béning-Saarbrucken line, completed in 1883, was promoted by Saar industrialists who owned mining and industrial properties in German Lorraine.

The only line built during this period and based solely on local considerations was completed in 1877 between Pagny-sur-Moselle and Longuyon, parallel to the 1871 border, to link the Nancy and Longwy industrial areas, since the Moselle valley route was now in German territory. In this case, local considerations were primarily political (location of the new border), since the westward extension of the Moselle iron ore field around Briey had not yet been discovered.

Traffic statistics for the railroads of Lorraine seem to support the idea that their economic importance was not fully achieved until the early years of the twentieth century. In 1878, the heaviest traffic took place on the Metz-Saarbrücken line (about 1.3 million tons), reflecting the active exchange of Saar coke for Lorraine iron ore. The Metz-Thionville line carried some 778,000 tons, and the Longwy-Luxembourg line about 650,000 tons. All the other lines carried less than 500,000 tons. This pattern reflects a fairly limited degree of interregional exchange, except for the Saar-Lorraine traffic.

The 1913 statistics reveal a completely different picture. In German Lorraine, about 8 million tons of iron ore were shipped to the Saar, Luxembourg, and the Ruhr; this meant a traffic of 5-7 million tons each for the Thionville-Koblenz and Thionville-Saarbrücken lines, since both of them also handled large volumes of coke from the Ruhr (a total of 4 million tons). In French Lorraine, the Mézières to Audun-le-Roman line, linking the French North and Northeast, carried a traffic of 7-8 million tons made up mostly of incoming coke and outgoing iron ore. The Nancy-Longwy line carried about 4.6 million tons, while traffic on the Paris-Nancy-Strasbourg line was comparatively light with 1.3 million tons only.

Growth of traffic on the railroads of Lorraine thus followed closely the stages of expansion of the region's steel industry. It was also encouraged by special rates on German railroads for iron ore and coke on the Lorraine-Ruhr line. But these rates, established in 1893 and 1901, granted greater transport cost reductions on iron ore than on coke, to the advantage of the Ruhr, and after 1901, the benefit of reduced rates on raw materials was gradually extended to other mining areas in Germany, thus wiping out any transport cost advantage which Lorraine had retained for the import of Ruhr coke. On the other hand, the steel industry of French Lorraine enjoyed very low rates for iron ore and coke transport prior to 1914. These rates were strongly degressive with distance.[12]

RAIL-VERSUS-CANAL COMPETITION IN LORRAINE

With all the advantages of the railroad, rail traffic did not monopolize the trade in heavy-industry raw materials during this period. Inland waterways still had a considerable role to play. In 1867, the Saar Coal Mines Canal carried some 473,000 tons of freight, including 352,000 tons of coke and 62,000 tons of iron ore; the average cost of transport per ton-km on this canal (3.90 francs) was competitive with equivalent railroad freight rates (7.64 francs). In 1873, the Marne-Rhine Canal carried a traffic of 611,000 tons, including 348,000 tons of coal and coke, 233,000 tons of iron ore, and some 30,000 tons of pig-iron, out of a total of some 990,000 tons of those products transported during that year in northeastern France. The same canal carried some 510,000 tons in 1891.[13] But inland waterways traffic was much less important in German Lorraine, where the predominance of the railroad was nearly total.

The rail-versus-waterway relationship in Lorraine during this period has been best summarized as follows: "From 1850 to 1914, the railroads had such a technical superiority over other means of transport that the latter's role seemed to be merely to serve as their complement. However, from the 1880s on, competition on the part of inland waterways became greater and greater for traffic in bulky commodities. ..."[14] Nevertheless, in the technical field, railroads were able in most cases to maintain their competitive superiority or equality, thanks to the technological progress brought to their operation.

From 1871 to 1918, each of the three States concerned with the canalization of the Moselle River undertook separate projects within the framework of their respective national interests. France lost its foothold and markets on the Rhine and was forced to reorient its Lorraine industry towards the west and south. Germany gained and retained control of the Moselle valley from Metz to Koblenz and integrated the Moselle iron and steel industry into its own economic

---

12 Schumacher, *Die westdeutsche Eisenindustrie*, p. 77; Alexander Tille, *Die Ausgleichung der Roheisenselbstkosten in Südwestdeutschland, Luxemburg und Niederrheinland-Westfalen, 1902-1907* (Saarbrücken: 1908); August Thyssen's pamphlet *Welche Gefahren entstehen durch den Saar- und Moselkanal* (1904); and *Bulletin de la Chambre de Commerce de Nancy* (March-April 1913), p. 264.

13 Auguste Pawlowski, "la voie d'eau Mer du Nord-Alsace," *RNIR* 9 (1931): 41-46; and Vadot, "La navigation sur la Moselle française dans le passé et dans l'avenir," *Der Ausbau der Mosel*, p. 83.

14 Degott, *La canalisation de la Moselle*, p. 383.

system. Four-fifths of the river's course in Germany ran through Prussia, which also included the Ruhr and Saar industrial regions. The remaining fifth was under the jurisdiction of the Alsace-Lorraine Reichsland, theoretically administered by the Imperial or federal government but actually treated like a dependency of the Kingdom of Prussia. Politically independent Luxembourg was economically integrated into the Zollverein, and its iron and steel industry was heavily dependent on German coal supplies; moreover, its sovereignty was limited to a short stretch of the river and had to be shared with Prussia, which had gained control of Luxembourg territory on the right bank of the Moselle in 1815. Its consent could therefore hardly have been denied to Prussian canalization projects.

The final terms of the surrender of Alsace-Lorraine to Germany were embodied in the Frankfurt Treaty of 1872 between France and Germany. Article 14 of the treaty stipulated that "each of the two parties will continue on its territory the work of canalizing the Moselle."[15] By July 1870, when the war broke out, France had completed all but the last 20 km of the canalized Moselle between Frouard and Metz. The new border bisected the river about 20 km south of Metz, so that the Germans had to carry on the unfinished project. Meanwhile, since the French had lost the northern Lorraine iron industry, the project had also lost its raison d'être for them: no longer was there any need to link Metz and Thionville with Paris and Strasbourg via the canalized Moselle and the Marne-Rhine Canal. Since they had also lost Strasbourg, the Rhône-Rhine Canal, built between 1804 and 1833 as a link between the Mediterranean and the Rhine valley, likewise fell into disuse, at least across the Franco-Alsatian border near Belfort.

Accordingly, France set out to replace the lost transport links. We have seen how this was done for the railroads. In the case of the waterways, not all the projects were carried out. One problem was to provide adequate transportation between the Longwy industrial area and northern France's coalfields, in order to rely less on imports of Belgian and German coal and to provide the North with iron ore and pig-iron from Lorraine as cheaply as possible. The route of this proposed canal (the Northeast Canal) was to follow the Chiers valley from Longwy to the Meuse at Mézières; from there, a canal would be built to Denain in the North. A branch canal was also planned between Longwy and Briey, where iron ore had been discovered in the 1880s. Owing to the hostility of the railroads and the shortage of government and private funds, this project, under study between 1872 and 1909, was never implemented.

While the Longwy-Briey industrial area of Lorraine did not succeed in obtaining canal links with northern France and Belgium, the Nancy region was more

15 Houpert, *La Moselle Navigable* (Metz: Chambre de Commerce de Metz, 1932), p. 50.

fortunate in this respect. Already provided with east-west connections through the Marne-Rhine Canal, it now became the vital crossroads of northeastern France, with a northward link to Belgium (the Canal de l'Est, northern branch, following the Meuse), and southward link to the Saône-Rhône corridor (the Canal de l'Est, southern branch, a revival of the old Moselle-Saône project). Both links were completed between 1874 and 1882.

The Canal de l'Est (northern branch) follows the Meuse from the Marne-Rhine Canal at Troussey (near Pagny-sur-Meuse) to Givet on the Franco-Belgian border. The waterway is made up partly of the improved river channel and partly of a lateral canal. It is 272 km long and includes 59 locks to overcome a difference in elevation of 149 m. It never carried a very large traffic because it served only one large industrial area (Nancy), and did not have any links with the coal mines and factories of northern France. But the upbound Belgian coal traffic and the downbound finished steel products shipments (from Nancy to Antwerp and Rotterdam) were fairly active during this period and have remained so down to the present (Table 6).

The Canal de l'Est (southern branch) follows essentially the route proposed by Lecreulx in 1776. Its total length from Toul to Corre is 147 km and it includes 100 locks to overcome a rise in elevation of 155 m followed by a drop of 140 m. From Toul, where it is linked to the Marne-Rhine Canal (through a 4 km-long side canal and one lock), to the steel town of Neuves-Maisons, 20 km upstream, the waterway follows the Moselle River except for five short side canals with locks to overcome a rise in elevation of 12 m.

Five kilometers above Neuves-Maisons, a 10 km-long branch canal (known as the Nancy branch) was built from the Canal de l'Est at Messein to the Marne-Rhine Canal at Laneuveville (an industrial suburb of Nancy). Five locks were built from Messein up to the divide to overcome a difference in elevation of 15 m, and 13 locks from the divide down to Laneuveville, for a drop of 40 m. This canal is supplied with water from the Moselle through a pumping station at Messein. It was to prove very helpful as a short-cut between the Neuves-Maisons industrial area and southeastern France on the one hand, and Strasbourg and the Saar on the other – at least after the return of Alsace-Lorraine to France in 1919 (Figure 3).

From Neuves-Maisons to Golbey (a suburb of Epinal), the waterway is a lateral canal which follows the Moselle, mostly along the left bank. This canal is 59 km long and includes 33 locks for a rise in elevation of 99 m. At Golbey, the main waterway leaves the Moselle valley and crosses the divide between Moselle and Saône: after a steep rise of 44 m with 15 locks in 3.5 km, the canal follows the Coney stream to the Saône, a drop of 140 m with 46 locks in 60.5 km. The waterway is fed by intakes from the Moselle and Coney, and across the divide by the Bouzey Reservoir (capacity: 7 million cubic meters), which is itself supplied with Moselle water through a 42-km-long ditch leaving the Moselle River at

Remiremont, above Epinal. The latter city is connected with the Canal de l'Est through a branch canal 3 km long. This branch runs along the right bank of the river and crosses it by means of an aqueduct (Plate 5) before running into the main waterway at Golbey. Above Epinal, the Moselle is a mountain stream; it is not navigable and is used only by the sawmilling and lumber industries of the Vosges.[16]

Traffic on the Canal de l'Est (southern branch) jumped from 325,000 tons in 1888 to 800,000 tons in 1913. But it seems that these figures refer to the Toul-Neuves-Maisons section which obviously received large volumes of coking coal from the Nancy Branch Canal and the Canal de l'Est (northern branch), for use by the iron and steel industry located along its banks. As for the section between Messein and the Saône, it was of little help to the steel industry because it served limited markets, just as the northern branch was of limited value because it had no direct link with other steel-producing basins than the Nancy industrial region.

It had been the purpose of the Freycinet waterways program, voted into law in 1879, to create a standard network of waterways by building new canals (and by improving rivers and existing canals to comparable standards) accessible to the so-called 280-ton péniches flamandes (Flemish barges) and having a set of standard dimensions — draft: 2 m, headroom: 3.70 m, surface width: 10.60 m, length of locks: 38.50 m, and width of locks: 5.20 m.[17] This network was designed to carry bulky low-cost commodities more cheaply than the railroads, and was also important because the existence of better waterways would put a brake on the railroad companies' demands for higher freight rates. The Canal de l'Est, which was part of this network, although it had been almost completed by the time this law was voted, did fulfill this dual purpose but fell short of expectations for reasons discussed above. Even after the completion of the Freycinet program, "the bulk of all water carriage in France was on the Seine, its tributaries and its ancillary canals including the Marne-Rhine."[18]

On the German side of the border, several factors, such as the combined opposition of the Prussian railroads, the Ruhr industrialists, and the Lorraine steelmakers, along with the open hostility of the Prussian government to the project (primarily for political and strategic reasons), worked against the implementation of the several Moselle canalization projects drawn up during this period. The Germans did abide by the clauses of the Frankfurt Treaty and continued the

16 Robert Vadot, "La modernisation du Canal de l'Est (Branche Sud)," *RNIR* 30, no. 6 (1958): 206-13.
17 Marcel Jouanique and Lucien Morice, *La navigation intérieure en France* (Paris: Presses Universitaires de France, 1951), p. 16.
18 Clapham, *Economic Development*, p. 352.

Plate 5 The Golbey aqueduct across the Moselle River near Epinal, Vosges, France, where the Canal de l'Est (southern branch) crosses the river and leaves its valley to join the Saône River. Author's photograph, 20 April 1965.

Plate 6 The Moselle River in the city of Metz, France: a view of Chambière Island. Author's photograph, 21 April 1965.

canalization work from the new border at Arnaville to Metz, a distance of 21.6 km, according to standards set by the French in 1867. But this section was not completed before June 1877, and the improvement of the river through Metz was not carried out (Plate 6). Finally, in 1880, the Alsace-Lorraine Parliament voted down the extension of the canalization work to Thionville.[19]

Actually, the Arnaville-Thionville waterway would have been uneconomical because its orientation was contrary to the prevailing (north and westward) traffic flows of the area during this period. River traffic on the Moselle across the border was insignificant compared to the Lagarde (border)-Strasbourg section of the Marne-Rhine Canal, as indicated in the following traffic data.

	Canalized Moselle (Arnaville-Metz)	Marne-Rhine Canal (Lagarde-Strasbourg)
1880:	14,319 tons	501,700 tons
1884:	18,819 tons	740,500 tons
1891:	34,236 tons	510,200 tons

Source: *Verhandlungen des Landesausschusses für Elsass-Lothringen: XIX Session* (Strasbourg: 1892).

The scant traffic on the Arnaville-Metz section of the Moselle explains why it was not included in the proposed bill concerning the improvement of waterways, submitted by the Alsace-Lorraine government to the Strasbourg Parliament in 1892. In the parliament's Budget Commission debates of 1894, the 6000-Mark annual appropriation for the maintenance and repair of lock gates on the same waterway was eliminated without opposition.

The canalization of the Moselle between Metz and Koblenz can be considered in three periods: 1880-1900, 1900-13, and 1914-18. In the first period,[20] following the introduction of the Thomas steel process, the canalization project was supported by the Ruhr industrialists as a means of providing cheap transport of Lorraine iron ore to their plants, by Spaeter of Koblenz who owned large mining concessions in Lorraine and would benefit from this trade, and by those Saar steelmakers whose plants were located along the Saar River and who would benefit from the canalization of both Moselle and Saar rivers (partly also because they owned local coal mines and were thus interested in exporting coking coal

---

19 M. Schlichting, "Canalisation der Mosel von Arnaville bis Metz," *Zeitschrift für Bauwesen* (Berlin) XXIV (1874): 149ff.; *Generalbericht an den Bezirkstag von Lothringen*, 1873, 1875, and 1877 (Metz, Buchdrückerei der Zeitung für Lothringen: same years); and *Verhandlungen des Landesausschusses für Elsass-Lothringen: VII. Session* (Strasbourg: 1880).

20 G. Berring, *Zur Kanalisierung der Mosel* (Metz: 1904); Schumacher, *Die westdeutsche Eisenindustrie*, p. 144; and Chambre de Commerce de Metz, *La Chambre de Commerce de Metz: 1815-1922* (Metz: 1922), p. 36.

downriver). The opponents were the Lorraine industrialists, who did not want to see their ore reserves tapped and depleted for the benefit of the Ruhr, and who were not ready to see the expansion of their steel capacity curtailed by adverse competitive conditions, and those Saar steelmakers who had no plants on the Saar River and would therefore gain very little by its canalization.

During this period, two projects were submitted to the German public works administration. The Friedel project of 1885, sponsored by the Koblenz Chamber of Commerce, was to have deepened and improved the river channel and included the building of 32 dams (7 in Lorraine, 4 on the Prussia-Luxembourg border, and 21 in Prussia), with a lateral lock at each dam. The average length of each pond was to be 9.3 km, and the average difference in elevation about 2.7 m, to be overcome both by the dams and by the natural slope of the river, since the ponds were not horizontal as in later projects. The improved waterway was designed for 250 to 300-ton barges, with possibilities for later deepening to 500-ton standards. The second project was drawn up in 1888 at the request of the German Ministry of Public Works. It included 42 dams (10 in Lorraine, 5 on the Prussia-Luxembourg border, and 27 in Prussia), the average length of each pond being 7.16 km and the average difference in elevation about 2.45 m. It was designed for 500- to 600-ton barges.

Traffic estimates for these projects were made twice during this period. In 1883, total traffic on the Moselle was estimated at 2,260,000 tons – of which 1 million tons of coke were upbound and 1,260,000 tons downbound (iron ore: 1 million t, pig-iron: 160,000 t, and finished products: 100,000 t). The 1889 traffic estimates (total traffic: 1,990,000 t) were a little less optimistic with respect to coal and coke shipments. In upbound traffic (640,000 t), coal and coke accounted for 600,000 tons, of which 300,000 went to Lorraine, 200,000 to Luxembourg, and 100,000 to France, and manganese for 40,000 t. In downbound traffic (1,350,000 t), iron ore accounted for 1.2 million tons, pig-iron for 120,000 tons, and finished products for 30,000 tons. These figures must not have looked too impressive to the authorities, because between 1893 and 1900, the latter seem to have lost all interest in the project. This sudden loss of interest may also have been partly due to the much reduced railroad rates for coal and iron ore put into effect in 1893.

During the second period (1900-13),[21] the Lorraine steelmakers dropped their opposition to the project and became its greatest supporters. Their industry had grown and prospered, and they needed cheaper transportation both to export their finished products and to import increasing volumes of coke in order to be

21 Schlenker, *Das Eisenhüttenwesen*, pp. 185 and 198; Schumacher, *Die westdeutsche Eisenindustrie*, pp. 38-9; Fernand Engerand, *Le fer sur une frontière et la politique métallurgique de l'Etat allemand* (Paris: 1919), pp. 95-100; and Verband für Kanalisierung der Mosel und der Saar, *Versammlung* (Metz: 1903), p. 15.

able to compete with the Ruhr producers. Likewise, the Saar industrialists who had opposed the project now sided with their Lorraine neighbors, with the understanding that the Saar River would also be canalized. Moreover, they owned a large number of plants in Lorraine. On the other hand, the heavy industry of the Ruhr, trying to preserve its own leading position on the German steel market, began to campaign vigorously against the canalization. It was importing an increasing percentage of its iron ore needs from Sweden, and it had a virtual monopoly over German coal production. In this opposition it was backed by the Prussian government, which also owned the railroads; the latter's traffic monopoly brought in handsome profits (derived from relatively high freight rates) and the government would not give those up. Supporters of the project often gave excessive railroad rates as their chief arguments in its favor. One of them wrote in 1904 that freight rates from Thionville to Koblenz and Hamburg on iron ore and semi-finished steel were proportionately higher than those from Thionville to Antwerp.[22] Another supporter claimed that "if one wants to build profit-earning waterways, one must admit as a consequence the loss in revenue for the railroads; if one wants to avoid such a loss, one will only be able to build uneconomical waterways."[23]

Actually, the volumes of raw materials and semi-finished products carried by the Prussian railroads between the Ruhr and Lorraine were so enormous that the canalization would not have meant such a drastic loss of traffic to them. It is also common to give strategic considerations as a major reason for the government's hostility to the project, although in fact the advantages of canalization far exceeded the drawbacks in this respect, especially in case of war. According to Degott: "The failure to canalize the Moselle during this period appears to result chiefly from the attitude of the Rheno-Westphalian steel concerns, whose competitive position with respect to the Lorraine steel industry and plans to extend their hegemony over the latter could have been impeded by the implementation of the project; their power enabled them to exert a decisive influence upon the Prussian State, which had to make the decision."[24]

During the first few years of the twentieth century, however, the Prussian government publicly showed great interest in the project. In 1900, it established in Trier a technical authority (Kanalbauamt) in charge of studying the possibilities of canalization by revising the earlier projects. Out of these studies came the Werneburg project (1903, revised in 1907). Initially, the number and dimensions of locks and dams were identical to those of the 1888 project; but for the first time, plans for the canalization of the Saar were also included, and the

22 Viktor Scharff, *Der Moselkanal: eine wirtschaftliche und politische Notwendigkeit* (Trier: 1904), p. 20.
23 Schumacher, *Die westdeutsche Eisenindustrie*, p. 97.
24 Degott, *La canalisation de la Moselle*, p. 625.

production of hydro-electric power was considered for the purpose of lighting the canal (for night traffic), maintaining the locks, and towing. Accordingly, it was planned to provide each dam with a 1000-hp generator. In the 1907 revision, the number of locks and dams was reduced from 42 to 39, each lock being 250 m long, 10.30 m wide, and 3.50 m deep. The average difference in elevation per pond was to be 2.57 m. The river channel would have been 40 m wide and 2.50 m deep, and would have allowed the passage of 1000-ton ("Rhine-Herne-Canal type") barges with reduced loads.

One traffic estimate, published in 1901, forecast a total traffic of 6,950,000 tons (iron ore: 2 million t; pig-iron, semi-finished and finished steel products: 1.7 million t; coke: 1,750,000 t; all other products: 1.5 million tons). A more detailed study carried out in 1907 and taking into account the canalization of the Saar came out with a total traffic estimate of 8,630,000 tons – 3,305,000 tons upbound (mostly Ruhr coke shipped to Lorraine) and 5,325,000 tons downbound (mostly Lorraine iron ore shipped to the Ruhr and Saar, pig-iron, semi-finished and finished products shipped from both Lorraine and Saar to the Rhineland). These estimates are much greater than those made during the 1880-1900 period and reflect the enormous expansion of the Lorraine and Saar steel industries after 1900.

It was perhaps the proposed canalization's contribution to this expansion which worried most Ruhr steelmakers. At any rate, in 1910, under pressure from them, the Prussian Minister of Public Works declared in Parliament that the canalization of the Moselle was "neither useful nor feasible"; he argued that no satisfactory answer had been found to the question of how pig-iron production costs in Lorraine, Luxembourg, the Saar, and the Ruhr would be affected by the project, and that the railroads were bound to suffer heavy losses if it were carried out. Oddly enough, no such arguments had been used in northwestern Germany, where the government had built an impressive network of waterways to link the Ruhr basin with the Rhine and the German North Sea coast.[25]

Seeing that the Prussian decision not to go through with the project was final, the industrialists and public authorities of Lorraine decided to petition the Strasbourg Parliament to reconsider the inland waterway links between Thionville and the French canal network to the south as an alternate solution to the Metz-Koblenz waterway. In 1911, the Alsace-Lorraine government undertook a study of the canalization of the Metz-Thionville section. The new waterway was planned for 300-ton barges; the navigable channel was to be 25 m wide and 2 m deep; six locks and dams were planned, the locks being 100 m long and 10.60 m wide. But Lorraine had to share with Alsace the legislative power in the

---

25 These arguments were forcefully defended in the German Parliament by Von Breitenbach, Prussian Minister of Public Works, on 7 April 1910 and 30 January 1914, and criticized in the *Königliche privilegierte Berliner Zeitung* of 5 December 1911.

Strasbourg Parliament. The Alsatians' primary concern was to have the Rhine improved between Mannheim and Strasbourg, and they were not ready to grant their Lorraine neighbors any competitive advantages at the expense of their own river traffic. Since the Alsatians had the absolute majority, the Metz-Thionville project was voted down in spite of heated parliamentary debates.

During the First World War period (1914-18),[26] the Germans greatly missed the availability of a navigable waterway between Lorraine and the Ruhr. All railroads were requisitioned for the transport of troops and military supplies. As a result, the steel plants of Luxembourg, the Saar, and Lorraine were deprived of coke and the Ruhr of Lorraine iron ore. From the very start of the war, the management of the Thyssen plant at Hagondange wrote to the railroads authority complaining about the shortages, which had caused the shutdown of the blast-furnaces, and requested shipments of trainloads of coke. This situation was to persist until the end of the war.

Under pressure from the military authorities, the Metz Chamber of Commerce, and the Saar iron and steel industry, the government reconsidered the canalization project in the spring of 1918. But the new study was not completed until 1922. It applied only to the section from the present Franco-German border to Koblenz, a distance of 241 km; it included 20 dams and locks, the latter being 255 m long and 12 m wide; the navigable channel was to be 40 m wide and 2.60 m deep; there were also plans to build 14 shelter ports. The new waterway would have been navigable for 1200-ton barges and its dams would have produced some 400 million kwh of electric power annually. In connection with the project, a newly formed corporation for navigation on the Moselle (Moselschiffahrt) tested existing navigation conditions on the river by sending a 200-ton barge from Koblenz to Metz. The experiment ended in failure, as the barge was shipwrecked before reaching its destination. The German government had done too little too late, for the Armistice of 1918 put an end to the project.

In Luxembourg, as in Prussia, the attitude of the government towards canalization projects was a reflection of the steel industry's stand on the matter. As in Lorraine, the Luxembourg steel industry, anxious to expand its own productive capacity in the face of competition from the Ruhr, was initially opposed to the canalization. Its location at a further distance from the river was an added factor of hostility on its part. Rather unexpectedly, however, the steel industry agreed to the project in 1904, precisely at a time when the Ruhr was beginning its opposition. As in the case of the Lorraine iron and steel industry, the Luxembourg steelmakers had expanded their production to such an extent that their

26 Association des Maîtres de Forges de Lorraine, *L'industrie sidérurgique en Lorraine: Comptes-rendus, 1919-1921* (Metz: Association des Maîtres de Forges de Lorraine, 1922), p. 69.

need for cheaper transportation (to import increasing amounts of coke and export their own products) had become acute. But the price for their agreements was a reduction of 2 marks per ton on Prussian railroad freight rates for shipments of coke from the Ruhr to Luxembourg. This reduction was obviously too great for the railroads to accept. In the event that the canalization of the Moselle would be carried out, Luxembourg had only one alternative if it did not want to rely exclusively upon rail transport. In the words of a 1907 official report on this matter: "If the reduction were not granted (and we very much fear that it will not be), there would be only one means left for the Luxembourg plants to compete with Lorraine and the Saar, namely to try and put themselves into the same situation as the latter with respect to canals, i.e., to be linked with the Moselle by means of an artificial canal."[27]

The author of the report argued that the construction of this canal would also benefit:

a the Prussian steelmakers in that they would have to pay lower transport costs on shipments of Luxembourg iron ore to the Ruhr;

b the Westphalian coal mines whose products would reach the Luxembourg steel basin more cheaply and would even be able to compete with the French and Belgian coal in the Longwy area;

c those Lorraine steel plants and iron mines located close to the Luxembourg border (Ottange, Audun-le-Tiche, Reckange) and close to the proposed canal.

This so-called Canal du Grand-Duché (Grand Duchy Canal), planned in 1906 by two French engineers, was to have followed the valley of the Chiers from the French-Luxembourg border to Differdange, a revival of an 1883 French project to extend the Meuse-Chiers (Northeast) Canal into Luxembourg. From Differdange, the canal would have crossed the divide into the Alzette valley, followed the latter for a short distance, and cut across in a straight line to the Moselle valley at Stadtbredimus, following in this last section the route of the old Mansfeld project. The canal was planned for 600-ton barge traffic.[28] The cost of the project would probably have been prohibitive, due to the large number of locks (32 for a total distance of 48 km) necessary to overcome the Moselle escarpment, and to difficulties in water supply.

Financial and technical difficulties notwithstanding, the Luxembourg steel industry soon reverted to its hostile attitude towards the canalization project. As in the case of Lorraine, the Luxembourg industry had largely been taken over by Ruhr capital during the first few years of the twentieth century: two of the

27 Paul Wurth, "Exposé de la situation des études au 1er octobre 1907" (Luxembourg: 1907), reprinted in *Le port de Mertert et la navigation de la Moselle* (Luxembourg: Société du Port Fluvial de Mertert, 1966), p. 40.
28 Pierre Hamer, "La recherche d'une solution au problème des transports fluviaux au Luxembourg" in *Le port de Mertert*, p. 15.

three largest plants (Differdange and Belval) were German-owned and their hostility towards the canalization project reflected the attitude of the Ruhr industrialists.

From 1871 to 1918, the problem of the canalization of the Moselle was tied to the development of the Lorraine iron and steel industry, which was in turn greatly influenced by the location of the 1871 border. The annexation of northern Lorraine to the German Empire provided the local iron and steel industry with a much larger national market than before and a customs-free supply of Ruhr coking coal. But in order for the industry to expand, cheap transportation was necessary. Fearing the competition of the more powerful Ruhr steelmakers, the Lorraine industrialists were at first opposed to the project; they were willing and able to pay the high freight rates charged by the Prussian railroads on coke shipments, and even so their production expanded. By 1900, when this expansion had reached a fairly high level, they looked for ways to increase their coke imports and their exports of pig-iron and semi-finished products and began to campaign in favor of the project. On the other hand, the Ruhr steelmakers were at first in favor of canalizing the river in order to increase their imports, first of iron ore, later of pig-iron, from Lorraine; after 1904, however, they became hostile to the project in an attempt to eliminate competition from Lorraine, Luxembourg, and the Saar. Not only did they succeed in convincing the Prussian government (which was anxious to protect its railroads from inland water transport competition in southwestern Germany) to shelve the project in 1910, but they also gradually took over a majority of the large Lorraine and Luxembourg steel plants, and began to build their own branch plants in Lorraine. Had the war not begun, it is likely that their attitude towards canalization would have become favorable once again. Their production was greatly hampered by the lack of adequate transport during the First World War, at which time the economic and strategic value of the proposed waterway became obvious to government and business alike.

The steel industry in the part of Lorraine which remained French lost a great number of markets along the Rhine; it had gained many of these during the free-trade period of the 1860s. After 1871, France closed its borders to all but the most vital commodity flows (iron ore shipments to Belgium, coal receipts from the Ruhr and Belgium), and the government adopted the glacis policy of discouraging the localization of heavy industry in vulnerable border areas. Nevertheless, the Freycinet public works program provided northeastern France with some economically valuable waterways such as the Canal de l'Est, which linked Belgium, southern Lorraine, and the Saône-Rhône corridor through the Meuse and Moselle valleys. But these waterways were small in size, and did not live up to expectations due to a combination of factors — railroad competition, protectionism in foreign trade, and a limited national market. The great expansion of heavy industrial production and inland water transport in the Low Countries and the German Empire stood in stark contrast with the relatively stagnant condition of the French economy (even though French Lorraine did become a major producer of pig-iron and crude steel during this period).

The possibilities of canalizing and improving the Moselle at this time were therefore based chiefly on three economic factors — the development of heavy industry, the growth of the railroad network, and various degrees of protectionism. Strategic considerations, although important, did not prevail except in wartime. Each government weighed the advantages and drawbacks of the project and tried to foresee how its implementation would affect the evolution of economic factors within the national context. The French chose to complete the canalization of the Moselle on their territory and to establish the Moselle-Saône link which had been planned since the Roman period. Germany and Luxembourg finally decided against canalization within their borders, since they felt that it would have harmed their steel industry and railroad traffic. In any case, national boundaries, especially the Franco-German one, played a very large role in determining each country's stand for or against the project.

INTER-WAR PROBLEMS AND GERMANY'S SECOND TRIUMPH: 1918-1945

In 1918, Germany lost the war and had to give Alsace-Lorraine back to France. Prussian hegemony over the Rhine basin ended and was replaced for a dozen years by the indirect control of the Allied powers (France, the United Kingdom, the United States, Italy, and Belgium). The terms of peace embodied in the Versailles Treaty (28 June 1919) reflect this shift in the balance of power. In the Central Rhine Commission, until then dominated by the riparian German states, the Allies held a majority of seats: 11 out of 19 (5 for France, which automatically included the President, and 2 each for the United Kingdom, Italy, and Belgium); Germany had only 4 seats, and the neutral nations the remaining 4 (2 each for the Netherlands and Switzerland). Each country had a number of votes equal to its number of seats, which meant that the German delegates would always be outvoted. Another reflection of the changed political situation was the shift of the Commission's headquarters from Mannheim to Strasbourg.[29]

The former international agreements concerning free navigation had two serious limitations: they did not extend the principle to craft of *all* nations, only to

---

29 "Traité de Versailles du 28 juin 1919: clauses relatives à la navigation du Rhin, de la Moselle, de la voie Rhin-Meuse et du Rhin supérieur" in Bonét-Maury, *Les Actes du Rhein et de la Moselle* (Strasbourg: les Editions de la Navigation du Rhin), pp. 15-16 (2nd ed.; 1957) and pp. 18-19 (3rd ed.: 1966).

those of riparian states; and the powers of the Central Rhine Commission were too limited and did not extend to the major Rhine tributaries, which the states concerned administered as they saw fit. The Versailles Treaty sought to broaden the Principle of Free Navigation by removing these limitations. Article 356 explicitly stated that "boats of all nations and their cargoes will enjoy the rights and privileges granted to boats belonging to Rhine navigation and to their cargoes." The Commission's powers were extended so that it would have the right to approve or reject any plan dealing with the improvement of navigation on the Rhine. As part of the peace settlement, France was given the right to demand from Germany the improvement of the river channel between Mannheim and Strasbourg, subject to the Commission's approval. Other French plans referred to in the treaty included the diversion of Rhine water into lateral shipping and irrigation canals in Alsace, and the building of dams on the Rhine between Basle and Strasbourg in order to regulate the river's discharge and produce hydro-electric power. On their part, the Belgians were anxious to secure a water link between the Rhine and the Meuse through their territory; the treaty allowed them to demand the implementation of this project from the Germans within 25 years after the treaty's ratification.

All the above-mentioned projects were subject to review by the Commission. The latter had thus been made more powerful by the Allies not only for the sake of more genuine free navigation, but also (and perhaps primarily) in order to put pressure on defeated Germany for the implementation of long overdue improvement projects. The geographical extension of the Commission's jurisdiction to most of the important waterways in the Rhine basin would have been a logical step towards the achievement of the Allies' dual purpose with respect to inland navigation. Article 362 of the treaty urged Germany not to oppose plans for extending the Commission's jurisdiction to the Rhine between Basle and Lake Constance, the Moselle from the Franco-German border to Koblenz, canalized sections of both rivers and lateral canals along them, and all other rivers in the Rhine basin listed in a new convention to be established between all states concerned. This convention on the "status of inland waterways of international interest," signed in Barcelona in 1921 under the auspices of the League of Nations, did extend equal treatment of river craft, on the basis of reciprocity, to all waterways under the jurisdiction of the signatory countries. But the Barcelona Convention was never put into effect because many countries, including Germany, the Netherlands, and Switzerland, refused to ratify it.

The Netherlands (which had been neutral in World War I) accepted the Versailles Treaty articles amending the Mannheim Convention only after signing two protocols in 1921 and 1923 in which they reserved their approval of the Commission's authority over Dutch waterways other than the Rhine and emphasized that "no State is bound to be responsible for the implementation of those [Commission] Resolutions to which it would deny its approval."[30] This limitation of the international organization's power, along with a general deterioration in international relations during the following years, would eventually lead to a complete halt in cooperation in the field of European inland navigation for a decade, after Nazi Germany and Fascist Italy walked out of the Commission in 1936.

After the return of Alsace-Lorraine to France, the Metz Chamber of Commerce voted a resolution on 8 March 1919, requesting the government to carry out the remainder of the 1867 Moselle canalization project (the Metz-Thionville section), with a draft of 2.50 m for 600-ton barge traffic, and the construction of river ports at Metz and Thionville. Two months later, while the Versailles Treaty was still being drafted, the chamber reminded te government that Germany had not respected its commitment to canalize the Moselle within its territory according to Article 14 of the 1872 Frankfurt Treaty, and expressed the following wish: "That in the conditions attached to the [Versailles] peace treaty, the conditions of implementing the canalization of the Moselle from Thionville to the Rhine, the cost of it to be borne in common by France and the other riparian States, be agreed upon and determined in advance; and that France be granted the right to demand the immediate execution of the project under those conditions, over a period not to exceed twenty years...."[31]

From an economic standpoint, this resolution had come at the wrong moment: France had just gone through an exhausting 4-year war; much heavy industry had been destroyed, especially in the North and in French Lorraine, and the reorientation of former German Lorraine and Luxembourg steel industries towards the French and Belgian markets was a difficult operation following the loss of Zollverein markets and the expulsion of the German technical cadres. There were numerous strikes and plant shutdowns caused by temporary shortages of coal. Moreover, the former German steel plants were sequestrated and sold at nominal cost to 5 large groups of French industrialists whose operations were in the North, around Paris, and in central France (except in the case of De Wendel). Most Lorraine plants thus became branches of larger operations in other parts of the country. This state of subordination would make them particularly vulnerable in times of crisis, when the main plants would monopolize the better part of a more limited market. In fact, the whole inter-war period was one of slow economic recovery followed by the Depression of the thirties. It took a decade to rebuild the steel plants in Meurthe-et-Moselle (the French Lorraine of

30 "Protocole relatif à l'adhésion des Pays-Bas aux modifications apportées par le Traité de Versailles à la Convention de Mannheim de 1868" in Bonét-Maury, *Les Actes*, pp. 19-20 (3rd ed.: 1966).
31 Chambre de Commerce de Metz, *Séance du 3 mai 1919* (Metz: Archives de la Chambre de Commerce, 1919).

1871-1918); and those in Moselle (the former German Lorraine) did not regain their 1913 production level until 1929, on the eve of the Depression. The French government's policies further contributed to the area's economic stagnation: they deliberately favored expansion of the North's heavy industry at the expense of the Northeast, primarily for strategic reasons.

The lack of dynamism of the Lorraine steel industry was thus due to an unfavorable economic situation, a limited national market, protectionism – especially during the Depression – on the part of most European countries, but above all to unfavorable conditions of transport. Not only did the French government discriminate against Lorraine and favor the North in its railroad freight rate policy, but it was also reluctant to push for the canalization of the Moselle for fear of orienting the Lorraine industry once more towards the Ruhr. Nor were the Germans anxious to stimulate Ruhr-Lorraine exchanges after 1918. They abolished preferential rates for coke shipments to Lorraine in 1919, and although these rates were re-introduced 5 years later, the reduction was not as large as in the case of coke shipments to German plants; this gap would widen with the introduction of revised preferential rates in 1933.

As a result, while iron ore-coke trade between Lorraine and Luxembourg on the one hand and the Saar[32] and Belgium on the other remained strong, the amount of German coke delivered to Lorraine decreased both in absolute terms and in relation to the total: from 5.9 out of 9.0 million tons in 1913 (65 per cent) to 3.9 out of 8.4 million tons in 1929 (45 per cent) and to 1.4 out of 4.8 million tons in 1938 (30 per cent). Likewise, export of Lorraine iron ore towards the Ruhr, which in 1913 accounted for 34 per cent out of a total of 13 million tons, had dropped to only 11 per cent of a nearly identical total in 1938, while the share of Swedish iron ore had gone up from 27 to 60 per cent.[33] This was understandable since all German iron ore concessions in Lorraine had been expropriated in 1919. According to Pounds: "In 1922, only 6 per cent of the pig-iron produced in Germany was from minette. This proportion changed very little; in 1928 it was still about 6 per cent. It rose to at most 8 per cent, but for the years 1937 to 1940 was 1 per cent or less."[34]

While it had recovered its political unity in 1918, Lorraine had also lost major markets with few economic compensations during the inter-war period. Increasing economic autarchy in Germany, coupled with a large-scale rearmament policy and an expansionistic nationalism in the thirties, forced the Lorraine steel industry to rely even more on the domestic market.

---

32 The Saar was separated from Germany in 1919 and placed under the trusteeship of the League of Nations; it remained an economic dependency of France until 1935, when its inhabitants voted overwhelmingly in a plebiscite to rejoin Germany.
33 *Stahl und Eisen* (7 May 1914): 812; and (17 October 1952): 1417.
34 Pounds, "Lorraine and the Ruhr," p. 159.

With a change in orientation also came the need for better means of transport towards the rest of France and Belgium. This explains the intensive campaign for the rapid completion of the Moselle Canal between Metz and Thionville, and for the revival of interest in other former projects. One of these was the Northeast Canal between Lorraine and Dunkirk, which had been under study from 1872 to 1909. Its former purpose had been to connect the Longwy-Luxembourg and Briey metallurgical basins with the coalfields of northern France, through the Chiers, Meuse, and Scheldt valleys. Now that the Moselle steel area had been regained by France, the public works administration decided in 1920 that the proposed canal would have to be extended to the Moselle River and that the best route under these circumstances would be through the Orne valley, a new canal across the Briey Plateau to the Meuse, the Canal de l'Est, the Ardennes Canal, the Aisne and Oise rivers, and the Canal du Nord (then under construction). This route was more southerly than the Scheldt-Chiers itinerary, and increased the total distance by some 70 km; it also avoided the Longwy area. But it was technically easier to build and would therefore have cost much less – 400 million francs instead of 650; but it too never went beyond the planning stage.

The Northeast Canal as it was planned in 1920 could only have been of value if it served as large an area as possible in the Briey and Moselle steel basins. For this reason, among others, the construction of the Moselle Canal from Metz to Thionville was necessary. Soon after the Versailles Treaty had been signed, the French Chamber of Deputies considered a "Draft Law concerning the works to be carried out in order to facilitate exchanges between the Saar Basin and Eastern France."[35] The proposed law included major improvements on the Marne-Rhine and Saar Coal Mines canals, and canalization of the Moselle and its tributaries, the Orne and Fentsch rivers, for 600-ton barges. But the Ministry of Public Works withdrew the proposals from parliament the following year, claiming that the matter required further study on its part, before the proposals could be voted into law.

In 1921, another draft law was submitted to parliament, aiming at "the improvement of the Marne-Rhine Canal, the Saar Coal Mines Canal, and the Moselle between Metz and (the section) downstream from Thionville."[36] The Moselle was to be canalized from Metz to Koenigsmacker, a distance of 46 km, partly by using the riverbed and partly by building lateral canals where necessary. The project was to include provision for later enlargement to 1200-ton capacity – the locks being 85 m long and 12 m wide; there were to be 3 dams and 6 locks. The 1921 project looked promising, the parliament turned it down because of its fairly high cost, at a time when the government was beset with financial difficulties.

35 Houpert, *La Moselle navigable*, p. 110.
36 *Ibid.*, p. 112.

A third proposal was made before parliament in 1925 by Guy De Wendel, Deputy of the Moselle. It also involved canalization of the river between Metz and Koenigsmacker, but was intended for 350-ton barges only, again with a provision for eventual enlargement to 1200-ton standards. Locks were to be 40 m long and 6 m wide, or about half the size of those provided for in the 1921 draft law. The cost of the project was also much lower — only about two-thirds of the estimate given in 1921. However, the Minister of Finance vetoed the proposal which could therefore not be debated by parliament.

In the meantime, the Minister of Public Works had suggested to the President of the Metz Chamber of Commerce, Humbert De Wendel (the steel magnate), the idea of forming a consortium for the improvement of the Moselle. This organization, founded in 1922, was made up of the Metz Chamber of Commerce, the Conseil Général of the Moselle, the municipalities of Metz and Thionville, and the Association Minière d'Alsace et de Lorraine. Its aim was to act as a pressure group or lobby to urge the government to proceed with the implementation of the project without delay. One of its functions was to raise enough funds (essentially through loans) for the project, since the public treasury refused to finance any large-scale undertaking of this kind. The consortium, along with the management of three major Lorraine steel plants (Hayange, Rombas, and Hagondange), finally came up with the solution to these financial problems.[37]

The solution was simple, and one wonders why no one had come up with it before 1926: the canal would be built with the financial, material, and labor resources which the Germans were bound to supply as part of the war reparations program. Germany actually built the canal, supplying all of the 2000 workers required in the project, and paying for most of the cost (192 million francs out of 220 million, the remainder being paid for by the local steelmakers). The project was approved by the presidential decree of 1928 and carried out between 1929 and 1932. Based on plans established in the 1920s, it was obviously more modern and better equipped for future expansion than the Frouard-Metz section built in the 1860s.

Unlike the latter's 13 locks for a distance of 60 km and a channel navigable for 280-ton barges only, the new CAMIFEMO (Canal des Mines de Fer de la Moselle) allowed the passage of 350-ton barges but was planned for future enlargement to 1200-ton standards (Plate 7). It included only 4 locks over a total distance of 32 km, the locks being 40.50 m long, 6 m wide, and 2.80 m deep. About two-thirds of the waterway used a lateral canal while the remaining third used the river channel proper which was 25 m wide. Two dams (at Argancy and Uckange) regulated the river's discharge. Five river ports were built on

37 *Ibid.*, pp. 110-15.

Plate 7 The Richemont thermal power plant on the CAMIFEMO at Richemont, Moselle, France, with a view of the work carried out for the enlargement of the canal. Author's photograph, 21 April 1965.

branch canals along the main waterway. The canal was run by a privately owned company, the Société du Canal des Mines de Fer de la Moselle, whose lease ran out on 31 December 1964, at which time the State took over its administration.

The CAMIFEMO could not have been expected to carry very large volumes of traffic when it was built, because it was a dead end for the first 32 years of operation, and also because of economic difficulties of the 1930s. However, in times of crisis, French waterways did better than railroads in holding their own. In 1920, the first "normal" year after World War I, total traffic on French waterways amounted to 23,284,000 tons (of which 3,295,000 t took place within Alsace-Lorraine) and 3173 million ton-km; it rose to a pre-World War II high of 53,295,000 tons (of which 9,386,000 t took place in Alsace-Lorraine) and 7266 million ton-km in 1930 (the highest ton-km total was reached in 1934 with 8377 million); by 1938, the last "normal year" before World War II, it had dropped somewhat – but not very much – to 45,018,000 tons (of which 8 million t took place in Alsace-Lorraine). This relative degree of prosperity was attributed to modernization of both infrastructure and equipment, especially in the North and Northeast. Undoubtedly, the new Moselle canal contributed greatly to the local economy, but it was only one small segment of the Alsace-Lorraine waterways network, whose share of total traffic never exceeded 18 per cent of the total during this period.[38]

The CAMIFEMO's promoters had argued that its chief aim would be "to link the (river) ports to be created with the mines and factories and to provide the latter with an outlet on the French inland waterways network."[39] This was understandable in view of the reorientation of Lorraine iron ore mines and steel plants away from German markets. A similar reorientation took place in Luxembourg, whose economy was separated from the Zollverein in 1919 and linked with Belgium in 1922.

The Luxembourg iron and steel industry was denied the German market and received little in exchange by joining the Belgium-Luxembourg Economic Union, since Belgium was itself a steel-exporting country. The French market had become saturated with the annexation of the Moselle steel plants, so that there was little prospect on that side. Therefore Luxembourg had to secure much cheaper means of transport than it had in order to compete with its neighbors on the export market.

The former Grand Duchy Canal project was revived in 1919, but lack of interest on the Germans' part to canalize the Moselle put an end to it for good. However, with the construction of the CAMIFEMO, Luxembourg could hope for an outlet to the south. Accordingly, the Luxembourg engineer Alphonse Kemp drew up a project to link the CAMIFEMO at Thionville with the Chiers valley through Bettembourg and Esch-sur-Alzette. This project gave the Luxembourg steel industry an outlet on the French inland waterways system and the possibility of having an alternative to the rail transport monopoly. In a roundabout way, it could thus reach Antwerp and Rotterdam by water.

The Kemp project was not the only one devised during the inter-war period in Luxembourg. In 1935, a more direct route to the Meuse was proposed, partly along the Chiers and partly through Belgian Luxembourg. The great disadvantage of this route was the fact that it did not serve the Longwy area. Besides, it was too costly to build because of serious technical difficulties. The same could be said of the Kemp project. Neither was carried out.

Having lost their economic interests in Lorraine, the Germans ceased to be interested in canalizing the Moselle after 1918. They did allow the completion of studies on their wartime canalization project between the French border and

---

38 Dominique Renouard, *Les transports de marchandises par fer, route et eau depuis 1960* (Paris: Fondation Nationale des Sciences Politiques, 1960), pp. 64-5; and France, Ministère de l'Equipement, ONN, *Statistique annuelle de la navigation intérieure,* Part I, Table B and Charts 1-2, pp. 16-19 (1965).

39 Houpert, *La Moselle navigable*, p. 162.

Koblenz, but at the same time, in 1921, the German government failed to include the Moselle in its program of river improvements. For several years thereafter, the German Moselle was used only by pleasure craft and some passenger cruise ships, of which there was a regular summertime service between Trier and Koblenz in the 1930s. In spite of hazardous navigation conditions, the Rhine shipping company Rhenus-Transport-G.m.b.H. launched regularly scheduled freight services on the Moselle in 1937, following a successful test run with a 225-ton barge between Koblenz and Schengen (Luxembourg). By the end of 1938, the company's barges had completed 60 round trips and carried 8300 tons of freight upstream (mostly sugar and flour) and 11,500 tons downstream (mostly plaster). One such trip in February 1938 included one tugboat and three barges, which successfully went up the Moselle from Koblenz to the Luxembourg border. The company also used nine 400 to 450-ton self-propelled barges. Navigation took place from October to April.[40]

This traffic, however modest, did not fail to attract the Reich government's interest, for in 1938, a new Moselle canalization project was drawn up by engineers Staat and Leblanc as part of a general study of German inland water transport resources. Originally, the Staat-Leblanc project stopped at the French border, and the Germans would administer navigation on the improved river as they saw fit. They were no longer in the Central Rhine Commission and Hitler was not interested in international cooperation, no matter how limited.

But by 1941, when the project was completed, Germany had once again annexed Alsace-Lorraine and had incorporated it into its wartime economic machine. German Lorraine and Luxembourg were both annexed to the Gau (province) of Saar-Palatinate. Four large German industrial groups were given ownership of the iron-and-steel plants in the Moselle: the Reichswerke Hermann Goering (Hayange, Moyeuvre, and Hagondange), Klöckner Werke (Knutange), Neunkirchener Stahlwerke (Rombas and Uckange), and Vereinigte Stahlwerke (Ottange). In occupied France, steel production (also made to work for the Reich) was divided into interregional production zones: the Longwy area industries were associated with the Ardennes ironworks, and the Briey and Nancy plants were oriented towards those in German Lorraine, while remaining in theory under the control of their former owners. Their production was deliberately slowed down by the occupation authorities and suffered severe shortages of coal and labor. But the productive capacity of the Lorraine steel plants was little damaged by wartime operations.[41]

---

40 A complete description of these activities is to be found in *Der Strom* (1938), published by Rhenus-Transport-G.m.b.H.
41 The most complete German description of Alsace-Lorraine's economy during World War II is found in A. Bleicher, *Elsass und Lothringen wirtschaftlich gesehen* (Berlin: 1942).

For the first time in its history, the Lorraine steel industry was not in competition with the Ruhr, strategic and military requirements having eliminated the problem of competition. The region was also granted the best preferential railroad rates on traffic to and from the Ruhr it had ever had. At the same time, the deep-draft canalization of the Moselle between Koblenz and Thionville was begun in earnest according to the Staat-Leblanc project. Most of the improvement was by dredging and removal of rocks from the river bottom so as to allow a navigable channel with a minimum depth of 1.70 m for at least 318 days a year and a minimum width of 40 m. The section between Trier and Thionville had to be canalized by means of 5 dams (at Trier, Grevenmacher, Palzem, Apach, and Koenigsmacker), and one dam was also to be built at Koblenz. Two of these dams were expected to produce hydro-electric power (Koblenz: 60 million kwh, and Trier: 25 million kwh per year). The new waterway upstream of the Koblenz dam was to be navigable for 1000-ton barges, but not for Rhine craft. However, provision was made for later improvements. Dredging and rock removal operations were carried out through December 1941, and work on the Koblenz dam through October 1944.[42]

The end of the war brought a halt to the project. France recovered Lorraine for the second time in 25 years and Luxembourg regained its independence. But the Germans' 1938-41 Moselle canalization project and the 350-ton CAMIFEMO completed in 1932, conceived in two completely separate and different political and economic contexts, were to remain the bases of post-war canalization studies leading to the implementation of the final project.

42 The Staat-Leblanc project was reconsidered by the public works department of the State of Rheinland-Pfalz under the French occupation government immediately following the war. For a discussion of this see chapter v.

V
European Integration and Prelude to the Final Project (1945-1956)

Following the defeat of Germany in 1945, traffic on most large European inland waterways dwindled to a fraction of its pre-war volume, since continuous Allied bombings had destroyed large manufacturing plants and river port installations along the Rhine and its major tributaries. If the volume and nature of traffic are reflections of the general level of economic activity, the almost complete ruin of Europe's economy in the late 1940s was faithfully reflected in the extremely low volume of traffic on most inland waterways. It took some 12 years for inland navigation to regain its pre-war level of activity, and this only after the implementation of the Marshall Plan, the creation of the European Coal and Steel Community (ECSC), and the beginnings of a continental transport policy started by the European Conference of Ministers of Transport (ECMT) (see the introduction for some comments about the latter).

Part of the reason for the relatively stagnant condition of post-war inland navigation was technological — too many barges were too old and not enough new ones were being built to replace the old ones, at least until several attempts to modernize the barge fleets were introduced. But much of the reason was — and still remains — political: there were (and still are) far too many obstacles to a genuinely free inland navigation in Europe. Nearly two centuries after the first attempts to remove them were made, much progress still remains to be achieved.

With respect to free inland navigation, it may even be said that there has been a regression since 1919, and even more since 1936, when Germany and Italy both walked out of the Central Rhine Commission. In the first place, the

Communist takeover in eastern Europe between 1944 and 1948 all but stopped river traffic between East and West, at least until very recently. The old Elbe, Oder, Vistula, and Danube International Commissions, which had all been by-products of the nineteenth-century concert européen, and whose raison d'être had ceased to exist after the Nazi invasions of 1939-40, were not revived after the war, at least not in their pre-war form. Instead, navigation on those rivers became subject to a series of bilateral agreements from which all Western non-riparian states (such as France and the United Kingdom) were excluded. The latter was also true of the Danube Commission, which was reconvened in Buda-pest in 1948, with only the Socialist riparian states as members; Austria (then under four-power occupation) and the US occupation zone of Germany were obviously unwelcome. Danubian trade became Eastward-oriented (essentially Soviet-oriented), and no attempt was made to foster genuine international co-operation. Matters were further complicated by the withdrawal of Yugoslavia from the Soviet camp in 1948 and by the "neutralization" (which actually meant Westward orientation) of Austria in 1955. But gradually, with the easing of East-West tensions, Danubian navigation regained some of its former impor-tance. Austria and West Germany were no longer denied membership in the Budapest Commission. Yugoslavia and Rumania launched a joint large-scale pro-ject, in 1964, to regulate channel flow on the Danube at the Iron Gates, where the level of the river is being raised and where hydro-electric power will be produced for the benefit of both countries. The Oder-Danube link, proposed by the ECMT in 1953, is no longer thought of as impossible, as both Poland and Czechoslovakia seek to intensify their trade with the lower Danube, southern Germany, and Austria. Finally, better relations between the East and West Ger-man governments are likely to bring about increased trade to the upper Elbe and the eastern half of the Mittelland Canal, thus restoring Hamburg's traditional river hinterland, which used to extend as far south as Prague and Pardubice in Czechoslovakia.

Given the post-war political, economic, and military situation in western Europe, one might have expected closer cooperation in the field of transport policy than has actually taken place. Of course, one should not underestimate the genuine efforts of the United Nations Economic Commission for Europe, the ECMT, the ECSC, and the EEC in this field over the past two decades. Their contribution has been worthwhile and indispensable, given the largely successful efforts at European integration (in the case of the 6 member States of the EEC, at least); but European integration cannot – and will not – progress any further without a comprehensive European transport policy.

In the field of inland navigation, much has been accomplished by the ECMT. The Central Rhine Commission has been less successful, if success is to be measured by concrete achievements. In this respect, the Allies could have used their power to enlarge the Commission's authority, but failed to do so, even though Germany had been soundly beaten and was in no bargaining position.

In fact, there was *no* German government from 1945 to 1949. Immediately following the end of the war, Germany was partitioned into four Allied military occupation zones: US, Soviet, British, and French. Most of the Elbe and Oder were included in the Soviet zone, and the Oder became the new Polish-East German border. The Rhine, Main, Neckar, upper Danube, and middle and lower Moselle valleys were all located in one or more of the three Western zones. The old German states (with the exception of Bavaria, Bremen, and Hamburg) were all dismantled and replaced by Regierungsbezirke in the Soviet zone and by Länder in the Western zones. The Saar was enlarged and detached from Germany for the second time in 25 years. Each zone was administered separately by a military high commissioner, though there was close cooperation between the US and British zonal administrations. The British controlled northern Germany except Hamburg, Bremen, and Bremerhaven, as well as the Land of Nordrhein-Westfalen (including the Ruhr, Cologne, Bonn, and Düsseldorf). The US controlled Hamburg, Bremen, Bremerhaven, the Land of Hessen (including Frankfurt), part of Wurtemberg (including Stuttgart), and Bavaria. The French controlled the Saar, the Land of Rheinland-Pfalz (including the entire German Moselle valley and the whole western bank of the Rhine south of Bonn), part of Wurtemberg, and Baden (including the German shore of Lake Constance). The Belgians, Dutch, Danes, and Canadians, although militarily present in West Germany, did not exercise any political control.

Given this situation, there had to be a way to regulate navigation on the Rhine. Fully aware of this, the Allies agreed on an interim solution, while Germany had no government of its own. In September 1945, informal discussions took place in London between representatives of the US, UK, France, Belgium, and the Netherlands "regarding the urgent need for immediate coordination of all activities undertaken with a view to restoring navigation on the Rhine."[1] At those meetings, it was agreed to reconvene the Central Rhine Commission as soon as possible. Accordingly, German riparian territory was to be represented by Allied liaison officers of the US, British and French military authorities, in addition to the Commission's regular member states (US, Britain, France, Belgium, Netherlands, and Switzerland; Italy never resumed its membership). Each member, including the military ones, was given one vote in the

1 "Accord de Londres du 5 novembre 1945 sur la reprise des travaux de la Commission Centrale du Rhin" (in English, with official French translation) in Bonét-Maury, *Les Actes du Rhin et de la Moselle*, 2nd ed. (Strasbourg: Les Editions de la Navigation du Rhin, 1957), pp. 22-3.

decisions. This was a drastic change in the statutes established by Article 355 of the Versailles Treaty of 1919.

The provisional structure of the Commission was as abnormal as the whole European political situation in the late 1940s, and some of its features were allowed to remain unchanged for 20 years, after many of the reasons for their establishment had disappeared. It is true that West Germany was admitted as a member in June 1950, several months after the creation of the Federal Republic. In April of that year, the member states and the Allied High Commissioners of Germany unanimously accepted Chancellor Konrad Adenauer's bid for bringing his country back into the organization. In his own words, "The [West German] Federal Government takes upon itself the obligation to abide by all the rights and duties set forth in the Mannheim Convention of 17 October 1868 and in the amendments added thereto, just as the present members [of the Commission are doing], as soon as it enters the Central Commission."[2]

In the 1945 London agreement, the presence of military members of the Commission was only seen as temporary, since (West) Germany would sooner or later recover its sovereignty. The presence of the US on the Commission was a direct result of this situation, and was also due to the heavy financial commitment undertaken by the US government under the Marshall Plan. When both reasons were no longer valid, the presence of the US delegate was no longer necessary; yet inexplicably, the US delegation did not resign from the Commission until 1 January 1965, some 10 years after West Germany had regained its complete political sovereignty and at a time when the Marshall Plan was nothing but a memory. The US presence could thus be attributed only to military considerations, since American troops were still present in considerable numbers in West Germany; however, one fails to see the logistic value of the Rhine and its tributaries today.

Likewise, British membership in the Commission could hardly be justified on other than historical grounds, i.e., the fact that the British had been among the chief promoters of the Vienna Closing Act in 1815. But if Britain was a member, why were other non-riparian states such as Luxembourg, Austria, Italy, or Sweden not invited to join? Surely their stake in the Rhine traffic and trade is at least as important as Britain's.

Far more serious than the validity of membership by the US or Britain in the Commission has been the continuing geographic limitation in the Commission's authority. Since 1945, its jurisdiction extends only from Basle to Krimpen and Gorinchem (Netherlands). The delta sector of the Dutch Rhine, though

2 "Lettre du 15 avril 1950 du Chancelier de la République Fédérale d'Allemagne (Konrad Adenauer) au Président de la Haute Commission Alliée (Général Sir Brian H. Robertson)" (French translation of the German original, presumably made by the editor) in Bonét-Maury, *Les Actes* (3rd ed.; 1966), p. 23.

theoretically regulated by certain clauses of the Vienna (1815), London (1839), and Mannheim (1868) agreements, is actually under the exclusive control of the Dutch Waterstaat (Ministry of Waterworks). Navigation on the upper Rhine between Basle and Lake Constance is regulated through a bilateral Swiss-German agreement, while France has only some limited rights to electric power produced by the dams in this sector.

The major tributaries of the Rhine are even less subject to international control than they have been in the past. There are no international regulations governing traffic on the Meuse, Scheldt, Main, and Neckar; the latter two are simply subject to the West German Binnenschiffahrtsgesetz (inland navigation law) of 1895, as amended in 1897, 1898, 1940, and 1943. The Meuse and Scheldt are subject to Dutch, Belgian, and French navigation laws within each country's respective boundaries, although each State guarantees free navigation on those rivers for barges of all nations. The new Scheldt-Rhine waterway between Antwerp and Moerdijk (Netherlands) is governed by the clauses of the 1963 Dutch-Belgian treaty, but the tributaries and distributaries of the Rhine in Holland remain under the exclusive authority of the Waterstaat.

The Moselle between Metz and Koblenz is therefore the only major Rhine tributary under an international authority, the Moselle Commission, established in 1962 according to the clauses of the Franco-German-Luxembourg Convention signed in 1956. The Moselle Convention and the Role of the Commission will be discussed later; but it must be noted at this point that there is as little possibility today as there was in 1919 to extend the Central Rhine Commission's authority over the Moselle. The reasons for this are different today: Luxembourg is not a member of the Central Rhine Commission, and navigation on the Moselle is not as free as that on the Rhine; it is subject to tolls. Finally, the 1956 Convention is essentially a bilateral Franco-German treaty, with some participation by Luxembourg, which was not a party to the preliminary negotiations.

The role of the Central Rhine Commission, whose task is to "debate on the proposals of riparian governments concerning the prosperity of navigation on the Rhine," and of the Moselle Commission, "responsible generally to look after the continuing prosperity of navigation on the Moselle in as much as possible," may seem vital to the progress of the European economy. Yet in the light of efforts towards economic integration, the two Commissions' influence has so far been surprisingly limited. In recent years their action has been supplemented by other international organizations more directly concerned with European integration, namely the ECSC (whose creation indirectly made possible the settlement of the Saar question and the signing of the Moselle Convention), the EEC, and the ECMT.

The first realistic attempt to solve the problem of European unification took place in 1950, at a time when Europe had hardly recovered from the war.

Politically, the continent was split in two by the Iron Curtain. Militarily, it was also divided, the Eastern countries being allied with Moscow and the Western countries with the US through NATO. Economically, the Marshall Plan was successfully solving the almost impossible problem of European recovery, but there were signs that steel production in most countries, after a spectacular 5-year rise, was levelling off due to saturated national markets whose purchasing power was still quite limited. Therefore, in view of a tense international political situation and bleak economic prospects, some way had to be found to give a sense of purpose back to the Europeans.

The only alternative to stagnation was economic integration of the continent. Many persons could be credited with integration plans, but two men stand out as architects of the first successful plan to integrate the European economy: Jean Monnet and Robert Schuman. Monnet, a well-known businessman (he owned a major cognac-producing firm), banker, and international civil servant, and the author of French post-war economic and regional planning, was an ardent European federalist who masterminded the coal and steel community plan. Schuman, his close ally, had been in turn Prime Minister, Finance Minister, and Foreign Minister of France between 1948 and 1950. His grounds for support were more personal than Monnet's: he was born in Luxembourg, where his parents had fled from Lorraine following the German occupation of Metz in 1871 — Metz being their native city. Thus, all his life, Schuman had to face the problem of divided loyalties: he studied and practiced law in Alsace-Lorraine, but in 1919 became Deputy of Metz in the French Parliament. Seeing his province artificially divided and his family needlessly split into French and German factions led him to believe that the only chance for a peaceful life in Europe's border regions lay in European unity. The only practical means to this end were economic, for other means had been tried before and all had failed.

Fully aware that power politics had been at the root of most European wars and conflicts, Monnet and Schuman sought a formula that would make war impossible between the Europeans. In his famous press conference of 9 May 1950 held at the Quai d'Orsay in Paris, Robert Schuman, as French Foreign Minister, exposed his government's plan in this respect. The key idea of his speech read as follows: "The French government proposes to place the whole Franco-German coal and steel production under a common High Authority, in an organization open to the participation of the other European countries."[3]

It is perhaps irrelevant to discuss here the other major points of the Schuman Plan, but it is worthwhile to summarize its aims. According to Brugmans: "The hour had come (to make a proposal) whose aim would be the United States of Europe, with Franco-German reconciliation as its hinge and a functional

---

3 Robert Schuman, "La déclaration du 9 mai 1950," reprinted in Henri Brugmans, *L'idée européenne: 1918-1965* (Bruges: Editions De Tempel, 1965), p. 273.

supranationality as its method. The press conference of 9 May 1950 ... crystalized this policy."[4]

The plan was defined by Schuman himself as "a leap into the unknown," but it had the backing of Europe's other leading statesmen, Konrad Adenauer of West Germany, Joseph Bech of Luxembourg, Paul-Henri Spaak of Belgium, and Alcide de Gasperi of Italy. In spite of some initial hesitation on the part of the European steelmakers, it gained overwhelming approval in France, West Germany, the Netherlands, Belgium, Luxembourg, and Italy. Britain declined to join: its Labour Party leaders, then in power, "were full of sympathy for Mr. Schuman's bold plan, but they really had to have more details before they could decide (and) commit themselves in advance to surrender certain fundamental rights."[5] Actually, the British were really not convinced that the coal and steel community plan would work. They kept their negative attitude for years, declined to attend the preliminary talks on the EEC Treaty in 1955-56, and decided to join the EEC only in 1961, and under such conditions that no EEC government could have accepted them. After the French veto to their entry in 1963 — determined largely by their own lack of willingness to "play by the rules of the game" — they turned away from the EEC for over 4 years. Finally, in May 1967, the Wilson government applied once more for membership, but the French were still hostile to British entry and the other members of the EEC expressed serious reservations about it at the beginning of 1969. Yet Robert Schuman had merely followed the ideological lead of Sir Winston Churchill who, in 1947 had clearly seen the need for a united Europe, and who its leaders should be, in the following terms: "The first step in the re-creation of the European family must be a partnership between France and Germany. In this way only can France recover the moral leadership of Europe. There can be no revival of Europe without a spiritually great France and a spiritually great Germany ... In all this urgent work, France and Germany must take the lead together."[6]

At any rate, 1950 was a crucial year for Europe; it marked the beginning of the vital Franco-German partnership advocated by Churchill and laid down the bases of the ECSC in concrete terms. Among the conditions for the establishment of the Community, Schuman emphasized the key role of free transportation: he insisted that "traffic in coal and steel between member countries (must) be immediately relieved of all customs duties and should not be subject to differential freight rates." Such categorical language on the part of the French Foreign Minister could not fail to impress France's 5 future partners, and negotiations towards a formal treaty began almost immediately.

4 *Ibid.*, p. 133.
5 J.H. Huizinga, *Confessions of a European in England* (London: 1958), p. 177.
6 Winston Churchill, "A speech at Zürich University, 19 September 1946," reprinted in Brugmans, *L'idée européenne*, pp. 265-6.

The Treaty of Paris, signed on 18 April 1951, established the ECSC, which began full operations in 1952. The terms of the treaty reflected faithfully Monnet's and Schuman's ideas. Most important of all, a High Authority with well-defined powers was granted the privilege of overruling national governments in certain economic matters related to coal and steel. However, in view of the fact that the satisfactory operation of the coal and steel market could not be achieved without a liberalization of transport rates and conditions, it is surprising how little attention transport questions were given in the text of the treaty. Without any doubt, agreement upon a common transport policy would have been a prerequisite to the formation of a single "European" coal and steel market. The failure to reach such an agreement is all the more unexplainable since the ECSC's High Authority has been very successful in many other fields of application of the Paris Treaty. We shall see that the lack of a common transport policy has also hampered the progress of the EEC.

The very beginning of the treaty lists some of the practices which would be ruled out upon establishment of the ECSC: among these we find "quantitative restrictions against the circulation of goods" and discriminatory practices "with regard to ... transport rates" (Article 4).[7]

The only article dealing specifically with transport (Article 70) grants very little power to the High Authority in this field. Given the ban on discriminatory practices, transport of coal and steel products between the various ECSC states was to be subject to "the rate regulations of all kinds applicable to domestic transport of the same good, provided that the latter follows the same route." All coal and steel transport rates (domestic and international) have to be published or provided to the High Authority, and "application of special domestic rate rebates in the interest of one or more producers of coal and steel is subject to the prior agreement of the High Authority"; this agreement may be "temporary or conditional." The same article, however, concludes by stating that commercial transport policy in its financial aspects and coordination or competition between various means of transport and alternate routes "remain subject to the legislative or regulatory texts in each of the member States."[8]

Under these circumstances, the ECSC's achievements in the field of transport policy are very modest. This situation has best been summarized in a study of the ECSC by Louis Lister: "The Community was rather successful in removing discriminations in the narrow sense. But it failed to make substantial progress in the field of harmonization because the ECSC proved to be too limited a basis for action and the power of decision was with the governments rather than with the High Authority. The creation of a partial economic union did not prove to

7 Service des Publications de la Communauté Européenne, *Traité instituant la Communauté Européenne du Charbon et de l'Acier* (Luxembourg: CEE, 1953), pp. 16-17.
8 *Ibid.*, pp. 81-2.

be an invitation to distort other parts of the economy for the sake of unifying two particular sectors."[9]

Lister's statement confirms the High Authority's own assessment of the situation, published in 1957 at a time when the coal and steel common market was just 4 years old: "The High Authority has come up against great difficulties in the transport field, which is under the competence of the governments, because its power under the Treaty is limited. The limitations of partial integration are particularly clear in this field."[10]

Both statements were perhaps made while too short a time period had elapsed since the establishment of the ECSC. A more accurate picture was drawn in a publication of the High Authority reviewing the achievements during the first decade of the Community's existence, recognizing both positive and negative aspects of ECSC policy in this field.[11]

The field in which ECSC transport policy met with the greatest success was rail transport, for which "discriminatory" freight rates were abolished. As a result, international rates were lowered considerably, domestic rates went up only very slightly, and those preferential rates which were temporarily allowed to remain in force were raised substantially. The most important single result of the abolition of discriminatory freight rates has been the growing tendency for industries to localize their plants in economically optimal sites. On the other hand, some well-established industries, whose localization depended primarily on the maintenance of national protectionism, have been hardest hit by the application of the ECSC treaty. As a result of this trend, the most favored regions have become those which were closest to one or more borders between ECSC states (Luxembourg, the Saar, Alsace, Lorraine). Many of these regions had a centuries-old tradition in trade and manufacturing, but their development had been hampered by the centralizing trends of each nation-state. In such regions, there was (and still is) a very urgent need for a supranational transport policy whose chief purpose would be to facilitate interregional trade and thus lead to maximum efficiency in manufacturing industries. Within this very recent context, the importance of the canalized Moselle River for the Lorraine economy in general and the iron and steel industry in particular becomes obvious. On the other hand, regions which happen to be peripheral in the European Community were hardest hit by the new treaty (western France, Pyrenees region, Bavaria, Siegerland).

This negative effect of the ECSC's transport decisions in some regions raises the question of their compatibility with the ECSC's avowed policy of aid to less-developed regions within the Community, since many of the peripheral

9 Louis Lister, *Europe's Coal and Steel Community* (New York: Praeger, 1960), p. 375.
10 CECA, Haute Autorité, *L'Europe en action* (Luxembourg: CECA, 1957).
11 CECA, Haute Autorité, *CECA 1952-1962: résultats, limites, perspectives* (Luxembourg: 1963), pp. 386-412.

regions have inadequate transport facilities, a low degree of industrialization, and a poorly developed urban hierarchy. However, the primary role of transport in the ECSC was not one of a catalyst for regional developemnt or désenclavement, but rather one of a tool for maximizing industrial production. Here perhaps lies the explanation of the failure of the ECSC to make very much progress in the field of transport. Only under a single Community executive authority can there be any hope of achieving a common transport policy.

Perhaps the greatest single failure of the ECSC High Authority in its transport policy has been in the field of inland navigation. With the purpose of eliminating discrepancies in freight rates between Rhine navigation and other waterways west of the Rhine, the so-called Petersberg Agreement was signed between the six ECSC states in Luxembourg in 1957, with Switzerland joining shortly thereafter. The agreement was never enforced because the various states were reluctant to give up their powers to legislate in this matter; many went even so far as to claim that the interference by the High Authority in Rhine navigation questions was contrary to the letter of the 1868 Mannheim Act. Even today, there is no cooperation in inland navigation comparable to what has been achieved in the case of the railroads.

Unfortunately, the "European spirit" has had its limits, and since 1945 most West European states have been very reluctant to surrender even the smallest parcel of their sovereignty in the field of inland navigation. If anything, the trend has been towards an increasing number of bilateral agreements based on the age-old principle of *do ut des* (mutual concessions, or "give-and-take"). The results of such an attitude were already made clear in the case of the Rhine, where the Central Commission's powers have been limited geographically. It will be seen later that the same has been true of the Moselle Commission.

It is not the object of this study to discuss the merits and shortcomings of the various European organizations in the field of transport policy. The case of the ECSC is taken here only as an example, but many of its shortcomings reappear in the case of the EEC. However, the transport policy of the ECSC deserves special mention since for example, transport of ECSC products represents nearly 60 per cent of total rail traffic in the Community.

Some spectacular progress has been registered in intra-Community trade, especially in the first 3 years of its existence, as shown by the data on railroad and inland waterways trade in ECSC Treaty products, the main increases occurring in scrap shipped to the steel industry of northwestern Italy from southern Germany and southeastern France, in coke shipped from Aachen and the Ruhr to Luxembourg, and in rolled-steel products shipped from Lorraine to southern Germany and from Luxembourg to Germany as a whole. Further evidence of great increases may be gathered from data on Franco-German trade in 1955 and 1965, even though these are not strictly comparable because the Saar was transferred from the French to the German customs area in 1959. Finally, traffic within certain regions, such as northeastern France, also increased considerably, as shown by data for 1956 and 1964 (Table 4). However, increases were by no means universal and in some cases there were substantial decreases in traffic, e.g., in shipments of Lorraine iron ore to the Saar between 1960 and 1963, at a time when the Saar, reunited with Germany, began importing large volumes of Swedish iron ore.

In conclusion, it might be said that the ECSC's action in liberalizing transport policies has had very little effect on river and road traffic, but has been very successful in cutting down railroad freight rates on ECSC Treaty products. A very good example of this progress is given in Table 5, which compares the transport cost of coke by rail from Gelsenkirchen (Ruhr) to Homécourt (Lorraine) at various dates between 1953 and 1964 with the market cost of coke. In 1953, a ton of coke cost 65 DM, including 26.54 DM for transportation, which thus made up 41 per cent of the total; in 1964, the cost of a ton of coke had risen to 85.60 DM while transportation costs had dropped to 15.92 DM, thus making up only 18.6 per cent of the total.

However, all has not been well with rail transport policy in the ECSC in recent years. During and since the construction of the canalized Moselle, the heavy industry of the Saar demanded the construction of the Saar-Pfalz-Kanal from Saarbrücken to the Rhine, in order to compensate for potential losses to be incurred on account of the canalization of the Moselle. In the meantime (for it is highly unlikely that the West German Federal government would agree to go through with such a costly project), the Deutsche Bundesbahn granted the Saar industry and coal mines some very low preferential rates, known as Als-ob-Tarife or "rates of potential competition." These rates affected some 5 million tons of coal, iron ore, and steel, and the rebates ranged from 15 to 54 per cent. On 12 January 1966, the EEC Commission condemned these rates, which it thought "are not rates of competition, even potential, but simply rates of subsidy forbidden by Article 80, Paragraph 1, of the Rome Treaty."[12]

It should not be very surprising that the ECSC did not achieve spectacular results in transport policy: the economic union applied to a limited range of products, whereas transport facilities are for the use of everyone and for trade in every product. But the Treaty of Rome establishing the EEC in 1957 did not really increase Community powers in the field of transport; nor did it overlap with the transport provisions of the ECSC Treaty. The Rome Treaty devotes very little attention to transport problems, which were apparently one of the major obstacles to the establishment of common ground rules for the Common Market which is still plagued today by a lack of common understanding in this field. This is unfortunate since there can be no true economic union without a uniform set of technical standards and economic policies in relation to transport.

12 See the article on the condemnation of the Als-ob-Tarife in *RNIR* **38**, no. 2 (1966): 47.

Since its founding in 1953, the ECMT unlike the "European Communities," has been a non-political, inter-governmental council of 18 European civil servants responsible for transport in their respective countries. Its main concern has been, as might be expected, to formulate sets of uniform technical standards for transport infrastructure in the countries concerned, resulting in an integrated "European transport network" for each of the modes of transport except airlines and maritime navigation. We have seen what came of its efforts in the field of inland navigation. On the surface, its record to date seems to be far more positive than the ECSC's, but it has no authority to enforce implementation of its resolutions by every one of its members. The road to European unity is a long one, even in such a non-political venture as the building of an inland waterway. The story of the final Moselle canalization project is essentially one of nearly two decades of bilateral bickering, bargaining, and give-and-take in the name of the "European spirit"!

PROMOTERS AND OPPONENTS OF THE CANALIZATION PROJECT

In France
It would certainly be a fascinating endeavor to tell the detailed story of how the present Moselle canalization project was finally accepted and carried out by all parties concerned. However, this would fall within the realm of international relations or diplomatic history rather than into that of historical economic geography. Therefore, this study concentrates on the essential aspects of this background, leaving to political scientist the task of sorting out the complex factors leading to implementation of the final project. Such a task warrants a detailed study in itself.

The benefit of hindsight with respect to the process of European economic and political integration leads one to the conclusion that even under the most favorable circumstances old ideas and principles are difficult to replace, no matter how valuable substitutes might be. It has already been stressed that one of the most significant (and to some, one of the most unfortunate) contributions of the French Revolution to the world as a whole, and to Europe in particular, has been the rise of nationalism as a result of the idea that the nation-state is the highest form of political sovereignty. This idea has had repercussions in all spheres of human endeavor, especially in the process of economic development and large-scale industrialization undergone by the European continent during the nineteenth century. Each nation developed its industrial potential and transport infrastructure within its own boundaries, as a function of its self-interest, and with little regard to policy repercussions on neighboring states. The proliferation of national economic policies led to the intensification of protectionist trade policies which never completely disappeared in spite of numerous attempts at encouraging free trade and tariff reductions. Even today, nearly 25 years after the enunciation of the Schuman Plan, over 20 years after the establishment of the coal and steel pool, and over 15 years after the birth of the Common Market, the peoples of Europe are reluctant to give up their respective national economic interests for the benefits to be derived from a supranational policy. The difficulties encountered in the case of the Moselle offer ample evidence that the road to unity is a very long one.

National rivalries were further complicated by divergent regional economic and political points of view. A brief survey of the various political attitudes with respect to the project will help to explain why it took almost a decade before the canalization was carried out. Even in France, where the benefits to be derived from the project were the greatest, opposition to it was strong and articulate in many instances. In contrast to the wholehearted support and initiative of Lorraine stood the energetic opposition of the SNCF (French railroads administration), Strasbourg, and Dunkirk.

The chief concern of Lorraine, in the immediate post-war years, was to rebuild its industrial potential, which had been heavily damaged during the war. The canalization, as a long-term project, was of little help in the reconstruction effort. Moreover, the Lorraine steelmakers were at first reluctant to commit themselves openly for fear of seeing their plants nationalized. This possibility was by no means excluded, since in 1945 the coal mines and part of the automobile industry (Renault) had been taken over by the state, then under heavy Communist pressure. Later, with the exclusion of Communists from the cabinet (1947), the establishment of the First Economic Plan (1947-53), and the beginnings of Marshall Plan aid (1948), the threat of nationalization vanished and the Lorraine steel industry became the foremost supporter of the project. Its interests were chiefly defended by the Metz Chamber of Commerce, which, as we have seen, had been a promoter of Moselle improvement and canalization projects since its creation in 1815.

Other local and regional authorities were also favorable to the project from the very start (Thionville Municipal Council, Comité Départemental du Plan, and Metz Municipal Council), but for two years the industrialists of the upper Moselle valley (upstream of Metz), whose interests were defended by the Nancy Chamber of Commerce, had serious reservations. They finally joined the ranks of the supporters with the understanding that the Moselle would be canalized from Metz to Neuves-Maisons (see Figure 2). Even before Nancy's support was secured, the project gained international support when in 1949, the Trier Chamber of Commerce organized a "Community of Chambers of Commerce interested in the canalization of the Moselle," with the participation of the Metz, Luxembourg, Saarbrücken, and Koblenz Chambers. Support for the project

2 shipments of Lorraine steel through Antwerp, excluding exports to French overseas territories, amounted to 353,750 tons, as opposed to 65,834 tons through Dunkirk in 1952, partly because of the shorter distance to the former (301 km instead of 406), and partly because of Antwerp's better harbor facilities;

3 Dunkirk would always be in a better position to handle steel shipments to the French overseas territories (230,000 tons in 1952) and pig-iron exports to England (150,000 tons), especially since it would always retain a near-monopoly of export from north French steel mills.[17]

Given certain traffic guarantees, obtained through successful negotiations between the Dunkirk Chamber of Commerce and the Lorraine steelmakers in June 1954, and the prospect of a new coastal steel mill to be built close to its harbor (USINOR, inaugurated in 1961; it is one of the largest plants of its kind), Dunkirk dropped its opposition to the canalization project.

In Germany

While opposition to the project in France itself was strong and well-organized, it could not compare with the violent anti-canalization campaigns in other countries, especially Germany. By 1954, German economic reconstruction was almost complete, and the Federal Republic's economy was once more dominated by the Ruhr industrialists. Moreover, the Allied occupation status was about to expire and West Germany was to become an equal partner in NATO in 1955. Fortunately for West Germany's neighbors, the country was governed by the late Konrad Adenauer, one of post-war Europe's leading statesmen, who with the help of Foreign Minister Von Brentano and Defense Minister Strauss, sold the "European idea" to his countrymen, just as Schuman and Monnet had done in France. Both countries were well aware that Franco-German cooperation and leadership would be the only guarantees for stability and prosperity in Europe. The Moselle question, so violently opposed by most West German economic circles, could either remain a bone of contention or become the symbol of a new and hopefully durable friendship.

The heavy industry of the Ruhr was never convinced of the economic justification of the project: even after all three governments concerned had openly expressed the wish to draft a final canalization Convention, the President of the Wirtschaftsvereinigung Eisen- und Stahlindustrie (Steelmakers' Association) spoke on behalf of the industry in the following terms: "Why should we agree willingly to the creation of a French route of penetration into Germany terri--tory? ... If Europe is going to derive benefits from it, let us be shown what Europe would gain by it. On the contrary, we argue that the true benefit would apply only to five or six Lorraine plants, and we do not see why we

17 *RNIR* **25** no. 21 (1953): 724-5.

Germans would be obliged to give some of our competitors specific weapons to allow them to come and sell their products on our markets."[18]

This was an attitude of no compromise, one which weighed heavily upon the decision-making process of the Federal government, and which systematically blocked any serious discussions and studies about the project. Numerous international meetings were held between 1952 and 1956, but in the minutes of every one of them one cannot fail to note the negative attitude of the German "experts," whose reasoning was often a mere blueprint of the Düsseldorf or Essen Chambers of Commerce arguments. Nor should the opposition of the German Rhine barge fleet during this period come as a surprise, for a large proportion of it was owned by Ruhr coal and steel interests. Once the waterway was inaugurated, however, German barge operators had no reason to complain, for their craft have consistently outnumbered those of other States on the Moselle (Tables 9 and 10). In any case, one cannot help but wonder about the sincerity of the Ruhr's concern: West Germany produces about twice as much steel as France, and its world export markets are far better developed. As for its own domestic markets, Moselle traffic data for the period 1 June 1964-31 December 1973 show that Lorraine steel products are exported to Germany in volumes which are small in comparison with exports overseas (this traffic pattern will be discussed later; see Tables 10-13). In our introduction, the idea of désenclavement of the Lorraine steel industry as one of the chief aims for the project has been advanced, but this does not mean that the West German steel industry would be victimized. If anything, increased competition for the Ruhr steelmakers, within the ECSC and on the world markets, could only benefit the customers.

Moreover, the Ruhr coal and steel complex, although by far the largest, is by no means the only important industrial region in West Germany. The Saar, whose heavy industry is also based on local coal supplies, was certainly more justified in its concern about the project. The economic history of the Saar, Lorraine, and Luxembourg has been a common one in many respects and for long periods of time, in spite of numerous boundary changes. In many ways, the three regions have complementary economies, but they also share the common problem of désenclavement in a European economic union. Before 1950, they could afford to supply their respective national economies with coal and steel within existing tariff barriers and with the existing transport infra-structures, although even then, competition was intense within their national frameworks. When the ECSC came into being, all three were faced with a paradoxical situation: they now had much larger export markets and were furtunate to be located in the geographic center of the Community; but

18 Interview granted by Mr. Schröder, President of the Wirtschaftsvereinigung, to the French industrial review *L'Usine Nouvelle* (12 January 1956): 7.

their lack of adequate transport facilities by comparison with other major industrial regions (Ruhr, northern France, Liège-Lower Belgian Meuse, Rotterdam-Europoort) made their situation precarious. Lorraine had canal and new electric railroad links with Paris, the north of France, and Alsace; Luxembourg had electric rail connections with France and the major Belgian centers (Brussels, Antwerp, and Liège); the Saar had no adequate connections with West Germany and an antiquated canal link (the Saar Coal Mines Canal, built in 1867) with Strasbourg. Its only good links were two electrified rail lines, to Metz and Thionville respectively.

The Saar has been a bone of contention between France and Germany since 1792, and has been controlled by one or the other alternatively several times. Yet it has always had close economic and cultural ties with Lorraine. Even today, shipments of Lorraine iron ore to the Saar are considerable and have decreased relatively little since the Saar was reincorporated into Germany in 1957. Occupied as part of the French zone of Germany in 1945, the Saar was granted a new Constitution on 14 December 1947 and a semi-autonomous political status on 1 January 1948, at which time its territory was enlarged to include the German bank of the Moselle River facing Luxembourg for a distance of 10 km north of the French border. For the first time since 1815, France and Germany did not have a common border in the Moselle valley or anywhere else in Lorraine.

In fact, the Saar was annexed to the French franc monetary zone and became an economic satellite of its southern neighbor, probably to a greater degree than in 1920-35. The Saar coal mines, once the property of the Prussian State, were transferred to the French-run Régie des Mines de la Sarre (renamed Saarbergwerke in 1955). The Saar government was pro-French until the 1955 plebiscite, and France took care of its foreign affairs, defense, customs, and monetary policies. In other words, this was a disguised form of territorial annexation which could hardly please the West German government after the latter had been granted full sovereignty by the Allies in 1954. It is no wonder, then, that the Saar government, steelmakers, coal mines, and Chamber of Commerce were outwardly in favor of the project and participated in the Consortium's activities in the early years of its existence. This attitude was dictated by political necessity and must be seen in the context described above. In 1954, the Consultative Assembly of the Council of Europe published lengthy and well-documented reports on the Saar and advanced the idea that it could be "Europeanized" or internationalized.

The French government considered that the alternative — returning the Saar to Germany — was a major sacrifice on its part. Realizing, however, that it might perhaps be the only solution in the long run (two-thirds of the Saar electorate had rejected the "European" status in the plebiscite of 25 October 1955, for this would have meant the continuation of the economic union with

France), the government decided to tie the two apparently unconnected issues of the Moselle canalization and the Saar status in its negotiations with Adenauer. The gamble succeeded, and it was a major diplomatic victory for the French, because the Saar had already chosen to return to Germany, whereas the Moselle question was still far from settled. Although a Franco-German Commission for the study of the project had worked several months (October 1955-February 1956) on reconciling the differences between the French and the Germans, the final report failed to include common conclusions and recommendations (its major findings will be discussed later). But it was used as a basis for the drafting of the Moselle canalization convention on 27 October 1956 in Luxembourg by the Foreign Ministers of France, West Germany, and Luxembourg.

In the meantime, after the plebiscite, the Saarlanders had come out strongly against the project. In the words of the Saarbrücken Chamber of Commerce, which represented the major coal and steel interests of the Saar: "With the canalization of the Moselle, the locational advantage held by Lorraine with respect to [its] markets to the west would be extended in all directions; this would surround the Saar factories on all sides and would isolate them ..."[19]

The Saar, faced with a fait accompli after the signature of the Moselle Convention, never gave up its opposition to the project. Luxembourg, as we shall see, was also placed in a difficult position but managed to obtain some concessions and became largely enthusiastic about the project. The Saar, also riparian to the Moselle, had decided, through the plebiscite of October 1955, to give up its autonomy and to transfer its decision-making powers (including those relating to transport infrastructure within its boundaries) to the West German Federal government.[20] The centralization of German inland waterways policy meant not only a drastic curtailment of the Länder's decision-making powers in their own affairs, but also a silencing of the pro-canalization lobby centered in the Land of Rheinland-Pfalz (through which most of the German Moselle flows), especially in the cities of Trier and Koblenz. For the Federal Transport Ministry was under heavy pressure from the Deutsche Bundesbahn (German Federal Railroads Authority) not to take any steps which would hurt its own traffic and thereby increase its already huge deficit. The Bundesbahn has been, to this day, the most outspoken adversary of the project.

At the end of 1953, when the pro-canalization forces were gaining strength, the Bundesbahn came out very strongly against the project in a 6-point declaration in which it summarized its position as follows:

19 *Mitteilungen der Handelskammer Saarbrücken* (10 May 1956): 390.
20 The West German Grundgesetz (Basic Law), its provisional constitution until the country is reunited, in force since 8 May 1949, transferred all West German waterways from state to federal administration, a departure from traditional practice.

1 The existing transport capacity was sufficient to cover the needs of future traffic requirements; therefore, there was no need to canalize the Moselle River.

2 It was by no means evident that, for most goods, river freight rates were lower than railroad freight rates.

3 Given the existing traffic and level of freight rates, the Bundesbahn estimated it would lose some 70 million DM ($18 million) a year, while all West European networks together would lose about 250 million DM ($65 million) a year, if the Moselle was to be canalized.

4 To the total cost of canalization, one would have to add the cost of new ports, warehouses, and barges; all this would entail the raising of considerable financial resources.

5 The implementation of the project could not be justified on economic grounds.

6 Within the ECSC, a lowering of railroad freight rates would make the project less attractive.

What is striking in this line of reasoning is the absence of any mention of electrification; on the contrary, the first point implies that since existing infrastructure was adequate it required no improvement for some years. The lack of constructive alternatives to the building of a new waterway was in sharp contrast to the attitude and action of the SNCF with respect to electrification.

To this categorical opposition by the Bundesbahn, the Consortium answered with the following 5 points:

1 Even the electrification of major rail lines was no substitute for a new deep-draft waterway.

2 In spite of the Bundesbahn's claims to the contrary, the canalized Moselle would bring about a lowering of transport costs, and even a reduction in the railroad's freight rates.

3 The Bundesbahn's claim that it would lose 70 million DM a year if the project were carried out was based on *French* traffic estimates for the canalized Moselle; if *German* traffic estimates were considered, the loss would only amount to 15 million DM ($4 million) a year.

4 The Rhine barge operators recognized that their craft would easily navigate on the canalized Moselle; therefore, there would be no need to build a whole fleet of new barges for that purpose.

5 The Bundesbahn made very large profits on the Moselle valley line — some 2 billion DM ($500 million) between 1918 and 1953; on the other hand, the new waterway would not necessarily kill all traffic on this line; moreover, the Lorraine steelmakers had always complained of excessive freight rates between Thionville and the Ruhr, and the proposed rate reductions in lieu of a canalized Moselle would hardly equal the savings to be made by using the deep-draft waterway; Lorraine would thus still have inadequate transport links,

104

while the Ruhr basin already enjoyed excellent rail, canal, and expressway connections to the Netherlands, Belgium, the Rhine and Main valleys, and the south German and Austrian markets.[21]

Even the opposition of the Bundesbahn, strong as it was, did not succeed in blocking the implementation of the project. It is here perhaps that the greatest credit could be given to Adenauer, who did not hesitate to go against his nation's economic interests in order to build a durable bridge of friendship and cooperation with the French. His countrymen owe him a lot, but other Europeans, especially the French, owe him even more. Nevertheless, one man's will cannot completely erase all prejudice and hostility. After the canalization was completed, the Bundesbahn kept on trying to fight by establishing so-called "competition rates" for shipments of coal from the Ruhr to Lorraine (Franco-German rate No. 1301): for example, on the Ruhr-Thionville line, transport costs per ton of coal decreased by 11 French francs ($2.25).[22]

In connection with the discussion of the achievements and shortcomings of the ECSC's High Authority in the field of transport, we have already discussed the effects of the coal and steel pool on railroad rates since 1953, along with the question of the Als-ob-Tarife (rates of potential competition). In recent years, the Bundesbahn has been seriously questioned by the High Authority as to the validity and fairness of its rate reductions. Likewise, the EEC Commission has consistently condemned the use of Als-ob-Tarife to protect regional economic interests as a violation of the Articles of both ECSC and EEC Treaties concerning the prohibition of discriminatory practices in transport rate policies within the Community, and such rates have undoubtedly slowed down the expected growth of Moselle traffic.[23]

In Luxembourg

Another reason for the Bundesbahn's continued hostility leads us to consider the attitude of the third country concerned, Luxembourg, which until September 1966 had no choice but to rely upon rail transport in its freight traffic. Between 1956 and 1964, Luxembourg nearly doubled its shipments of rolled-steel products to Germany (including the Saar), from 380,000 to 623,000 tons, most of it having used the rolling stock and equipment of the Bundesbahn. Following the canalization project's completion, and even before work had started on the Luxembourg Moselle port of Mertert, the Bundesbahn, fearful of traffic losses, substantially reduced its rates on steel products

21 "La canalisation de la Moselle: mise au point du Consortium pour l'aménagement de la Moselle sur la prise de position de la *Bundesbahn*," *RNIR* **26**, no. 1(1954): 17-19.
22 Information kindly supplied by Mr. I. Debois, Director, Direction des Transports, Direction Générale Economie et Energie, High Authority of the ECSC, Luxembourg, in a letter to the author dated 13 August 1965.
23 *RNIR* **38**, no. 2 (1966):47.

shipped from Luxembourg to Germany (German-Luxembourg rate No. 5101), so that the transport cost for a ton of steel-plate from Esch-sur-Alzette to Mannheim was reduced by 70 LF ($1.40).[24]

In fact, Luxembourg had a good reason to oppose the project: even if the latter would be carried out, the Grand Duchy's steel industry would not gain by it unless some way could be found to link the steel-producing Alzette and Chiers valleys to the new waterway, a distance of 49 km. We have seen that in the past numerous projects for canal links had been under study, starting with Mansfeld's project in the seventeenth century. But even today such a canal would be too costly to build. The only alternative for Luxembourg was therefore to build a port on the Moselle and link it by electric railway to the steel basin. In this way, the CFL (Société Nationale des Chemins de Fer Luxembourgeois, the country's railroad company) would derive added benefits from increased traffic over its own right-of-way. But the CFL was initially opposed to the project, possibly because of its economic and financial solidarity with the French and German railroads. It depends on them not only for the bulk of its traffic, but also for financial and technical assistance (until 1957 the SNCF owned a large amount of CFL stock). In 1953, the Luxembourg Prime Minister declared that "our rail traffic would lose 5 million LF ($100,000) a year on account of the implementation of this project."[25] These fears were not completely without foundation. The CFL assumed that the transit traffic on the Lorraine-Antwerp rail connection (which goes through Luxembourg) would be completely lost to the new waterway, and that another possible traffic diversion might occur on the line used for coke shipments from Wanne-Eickel (Ruhr) to Esch-sur-Alzette, a traffic which instead of using the northeastern line (through Trier and Wasserbillig), might then use the Moselle to Thionville line and the short rail line from Thionville to Esch via Audun-le-Tiche, lying mostly within French territory. Total loss from such traffic diversions was estimated at 21.4 million LF ($428,000) a year in the 1956 Wehenkel Report to Parliament with regard to the approval of the Moselle canalization convention. It must be stressed that these arguments are part of a text which is on the whole favorable to the project,[26] and the same report came up with a gross gain of 37.4 million LF ($748,000) a year and concluded that

---

24 Letter of Mr. I. Debois, 13 August 1965 (see note 22).
25 In an interview granted to the Metz newspaper *Le Républicain Lorrain* on 18 October 1953.
26 Antoine Wehenkel, Rapporteur, "Projet de Loi portant approbation de la Convention entre le Grand-Duché de Luxembourg, la République Fédérale d'Allemagne et la République Française au sujet de la canalisation de la Moselle et du Protocole franco-luxembourgeois relatif au règlement de certaines questions liées à cette Convention, signés à Luxembourg, Chambre des Députés, Session ordinaire de 1956-1957, *Document No. 606-1* (26 December 1956): 9.

"the influence of the canalization upon the financial situation can be nothing but favorable; at worst, one could say that it constitutes for our national rail-roads company a break-even operation." From this statement it is quite clear that the CFL had given up its solidarity with other railroads in order to make the most of the new situation: "[West Germany, France, and Belgium] have certainly other means to solve the difficulties brought about by [the new waterway] to their railroad networks. One cannot really ask our CFL and our railroad workers, who can only derive benefits from the canalization, to com-mit harakiri in a spirit of solidarity with respect to their foreign colleagues."[27]

This sudden burst of enthusiasm for a cause which the Luxembourg govern-ment first defended and later opposed was explained in the report itself. Al-though a riparian power and one of the first advocates of the canalization project, Luxembourg had been left out of the bilateral Franco-German discus-sions which had begun in 1953. To the very end, the two big countries ignored their small neighbor and after agreeing upon the terms of the Conven-tion faced the Grand Duchy with a fait accompli, upon which Joseph Bech, Luxembourg's Foreign Minister and a leading European statesman, told the French that his country was no longer the Département des Forêts,[28] and in-sisted on compensation to be paid for fully by the French. His argument, re-stated in the Wehenkel Report, was that in order to take advantage of the new waterway, Luxembourg would have to build the river port at Mertert (see Figure 4), which would cost some 300-350 million LF ($6-7 million) and modernize and electrify the Rodange-Esch-Bettembourg-Wasserbillig rail line, linking it with the port installations at Mertert; the cost of these railroad im-provements would amount to 120 million LF ($2.4 million). Luxembourg would thus have to spend 420-470 million LF ($8.4-9.4 million), a consider-able sum of money for a small country with 325,000 inhabitants. France being the chief beneficiary of the project would have to pay for these com-pensations in exchange of which Luxembourg would agree to place itself in a disadvantageous competitive position.vis-à-vis its southern neighbor.

But a face-saving way had to be found for France to agree, for it was diffi-cult at this time for the French government to come up with large sums of foreign exchange, engaged as it had been for a decade in two costly colonial wars for which it had spent large amounts of money in military weapons and supplies. An acceptable answer was found: France would supply the CFL with

27 *Ibid.*, p. 10.
28 Along with Belgium, southern Holland, and the west bank of the Rhine in Germany, Luxembourg was incorporated into the French Republic between 1792 and 1797 and remained part of France until 1815 under the name of Département des Forêts, as all the newly-acquired territories were divided into Départements to conform to similar French administrative units.

20 electric locomotives of the latest design between 1 July 1957 and the end of 1959; these were worth 264 million LF altogether ($4.28 million); moreover, on 1 January 1957, the French government would relinquish all of the capital, amortization, interests, etc., held by it in the CFL since 1946, while maintaining all other rights in the latter. This meant turning over some 186 million LF ($3.72 million) to the Grand-Duchy, which thus received a total of 450 million LF ($9 million) from the French government, a sum equal to the cost of building the port of Mertert and improving the rail lines leading to it from the steel basin. These concessions were attached to the Moselle Convention as a bilateral Protocol signed by the two countries' Foreign Ministers, Pineau and Bech, at Luxembourg on 27 October 1956.[29] They may seem to have been mere devices to appease Luxembourg by recognizing its rights as a sovereign State. But they also meant real benefits to the CFL and to the Grand Duchy's steel industry. The gains to the railroads were best summarized by Victor Bodson, then Minister of Transport of Luxembourg, in the following words:

As a result of the creation of the port of Mertert, our railroads will benefit from additional revenues. ... For our exports, there will be a shift in traffic towards the port of Mertert. This traffic will take place over a Luxembourg route some 50-60 km long instead of the current 20 km [route]. This longer route will bring in added revenues for our railroads.

Despite lower freight rates and with the same volume of traffic, railroad revenues will increase by 2 per cent or by 20-24 million LF [$400,000-480,000]. ... The net gain will be 13 to 17 million LF [$260,000-340,000], or a little over one per cent of total revenues.[30]

The attitude of the Luxembourg steel industry, the country's largest single economic activity (The Grand Duchy produces more steel per capita than any other country in the world), followed closely that of the CFL in its changing mood. ARBED (Aciéries Réunies de Bourbach, Eich et Dudelange), the country's largest steel producer and one of Europe's largest, through the action of its President, Henri Welter, finally became one of the project's most dedicated supporters after the French had given Luxembourg adequate financial satisfaction. Yet government sources had forecast that Luxembourg's steelmakers

---

29 Wehenkel, "Projet de Loi," pp. 8-9; and "Protocole entre le Gouvernement de la République Française et le Gouvernement du Grand-Duché de Luxembourg relatif au règlement de certaines questions liées à la Convention franco-germano-luxembourgeoise relative à la canalisation de la Moselle," *La Documentation Française: Notes et Etudes Documentaires*, No. 2270 (9 March 1957), p. 19.

30 Victor Bodson, "Le Luxembourg et la canalisation de la Moselle," in *La Moselle: son passé, son avenir* (Schwebsingen: Imprinerie Bourg-Bourger, 1958), p. 53.

would lose some 150 million LF ($3 million) a year to those steel plants located in Lorraine, on account of a more intensive use of the improved Moselle by the Lorraine plants.

The support of the Grand Duchy's steel industry became vital when the parliament voted the law of 22 July 1963 "concerning the construction and operation of a river port on the Moselle."[31] This law provided a 99-year lease for the construction and operation of the port by the Société du Port Fluvial de Mertert S.A., a joint-stock corporation, 50 per cent of whose stock was owned by the state, 40 per cent by the steel industry, and 10 per cent by two large Luxembourg banks. The corporation's initial capital, provided by the state, was only 5 million LF ($100,000), but it was empowered to raise up to 400 million LF ($8 million) plus interest and service charges, through long-term borrowing and governmental credits, including the state's credit vis-à-vis the CFL, which included property rights over the 20 French-built electric locomotives and some 23 million LF ($460,000) which the state had paid as import duties on the latter. The financial assets held by the steel industry in the corporation are thus enormous.

Aside from its great financial commitment, the Luxembourg steel industry has some definite interests with respect to traffic on the Moselle. According to Welter, such interests rest on the assumption that the port of Mertert, in conjunction with a modernized, electrified railroad network, would contribute to offsetting the industry's locational disadvantage in regard to the Lorraine steel plants, not so much through an immediate reduction of transport costs for raw materials and finished rolled-steel products, as through the creation of new or increased traffic flows made possible only by the existence of the new waterway.

Among these, Welter mentions: 1, high-grade iron ore imports from Africa and Brazil to diminish the industry's exclusive reliance on domestic or French minette; 2, larger volumes of coke imports from the Ruhr and Belgium; 3, larger volumes of exports of steel products to overseas markets and especially to the other ECSC member states; 4, much better prospects for exports of blast-furnace granulated slag to West German cement plants; and 5, increased volumes of Thomas slag to be shipped to the other ECSC member states. How much of this traffic will use the combined water-rail route through Mertert remains to be seen. Welter himself admits that his assumptions rely at best on educated guesses.

31 Henri Welter, "L'attitude de l'industrie sidérurgique luxembourgeoise face à la canalisation de la Moselle et à la construction du port de Mertert" in *Le port de Mertert et la navigation de la Moselle* (Luxembourg: Société du Port Fluvial de Mertert, 1966), pp. 83-7; "Loi du 22 juillet 1963 relative à l'aménagement et à l'exploitation d'un port fluvial sur la Moselle," Luxembourg, Chambre des Députés, Session ordinaire du 1962-1963, Document No. 868; "Les répercussions de la canalisation de la Moselle sur l'économie luxembourgeoise," *RNIR* 28, no. 5 (1956): 172-3.

Work started on the port facilities on 13 February 1964 (when the canalization proper had almost been completed) and the dock was completed on 3 December 1965. The full facilities were inaugurated on 1 September 1966. Therefore, the few traffic statistics already available are insufficient to make any sound predictions as to how greatly Luxembourg's steel industry will benefit from the canalized Moselle. What remains certain, however, is that Luxembourg could not remain isolated in Europe when all around it, in Belgium, France, and West Germany, heavy industry was being offered improved means of transport. Since about 96 per cent of the Grand Duchy's steel production is exported, the country could not afford to keep on relying exclusively on rail links with the Ruhr, the Saar, Lorraine, Antwerp, and Liège. The désenclavement of its economy required alternate means of transport, provided that these were not financially prohibitive.

In Belgium and the Netherlands

It is therefore logical to assume that Belgium would have the most to lose from the Moselle canalization project, with the port of Antwerp and the SNCB (Société Nationale des Chemins de Fer Belges, the Belgian National Railroads Administration) hardest hit. The Belgians had all the more reason to be concerned since Luxembourg, though associated with Belgium in an economic union since 1922, had gone its own way in the question of the Moselle without prior consultations with its larger partner. This "breach of faith" did contribute to Belgium's hostility towards the project, but one must look for economic rather than psychological reasons in order to understand this attitude.

In theory at least, Belgium was not directly concerned with a project which was not located on its territory, so that even though it had some reason to be concerned, its opposition was not very vocal. The Belgian steel industry, being located around Charleroi, Ghent, Liège, and the Campine, was well-provided with far better waterway and rail connections to Antwerp than its Luxembourg competitors, and had therefore very little reason to worry. On the other hand, the SNCB pretended it would lose a great amount of traffic on its Liège-Trois-vierges-(Luxembourg) line (transport of coal from the Belgian provinces of Limburg and Liège to the Luxembourg steel basin) and even more on its Antwerp-Brussels-Namur-Arlon-Athus-(Differdange) line (transport of rolled-steel products from Luxembourg to Charleroi, Brussels, and Antwerp). Much of Luxembourg's Antwerp-bound traffic would go via the Moselle, Rhine, and Scheldt-Rhine waterway, while Belgian coalfields would lose some of their Luxembourg markets to the Dutch Limburg coal producers who were closer to the Meuse-Rhine-Moselle route. The Antwerp-Arlon line is also the traditional outlet for steel products shipped from Lorraine to Antwerp; with the canalized Moselle, such products might at least partly travel by inland waterways, either to Antwerp or to Rotterdam. Finally, even part of the French iron ore shipments to Belgium might possibly use the new waterway, although the Belgian steel industry has a growing tendency to import overseas high-grade ores. Of all the railroad networks discussed, the Belgian one had thus the most to lose from the implementation of the project. But surprisingly enough, the Belgian government, which owns the SNCB, did not openly oppose the project, although it showed its concern by trying to participate in the canalization discussions, with little success. According to the RNIR (10 December 1954), Mr Anseele, Belgian Communications Minister, declared in parliament that the government would adopt a position of hostility (like his own) to the project; but following these threats, the Lorraine steelmakers began to divert some of their export traffic from Antwerp to Rotterdam. Fearful of alienating the powerful Antwerp Port Authority, the Belgian government became more cautious and ceased its open opposition to the project.

The port of Antwerp itself reacted to the project in a more subtle way. Prior to World War II, Antwerp was the leading export outlet for Lorraine steel, a position which it lost to Dunkirk in the 1950s. When the Moselle project was being discussed, Antwerp feared severe traffic losses to Rotterdam, which is the more logical outlet for the Rhine-Moselle traffic. As a countermove, Antwerp and most leading Belgian economic experts (including the geographer A. Delmer) played upon the vital need to canalize the Meuse in Belgium and France and link it to Lorraine and Luxembourg via the Chiers valley, this reviving once again the old North-East canal project from Sedan to Longwy.[32]

Later, after the project was approved and carried through, Antwerp ceased its opposition and even became optimistic. Using the argument that it was the best equipped North Sea port for the export of steel products (Rotterdam being more specialized in petroleum imports), the Antwerp Port Authority claimed that its traffic with Lorraine would probably increase with the canalization of the Moselle in spite of the added competition of Rotterdam. One author wrote (perhaps somewhat optimistically): "Antwerp, seaport of the Moselle? Of course, as soon as the canalization of the Moselle is completed."[33] We will see that traffic data for the new waterway's early years of operation have confirmed Antwerp's leading position in the export of Lorraine steel products.

A few words must be added concerning Dutch attitudes towards the project. Of course, the Rotterdam port authorities were at least as optimistic and confident as those in Antwerp that Rotterdam would become the one and only gateway to Moselle export traffic. The compilation of early traffic data shows that such optimism could not be entirely justified, since the port of Antwerp did

32 Robert Planchar, *Le rôle économique de la Meuse dans la CECA* (Liège: Université de Liège, 1955), p. 129; A. Delmer, "Les voies navigables reliant la Mer du Nord à la Méditerranée: voies alsacienne, lorraine, ardennaise," *Bulletin de la Société Belge d'Etudes Géographiques* 31, no. 1 (1962): 86.

33 L. Roman, "Anvers, port de mer de la Moselle," *RNIR* 33, no. 10 (1961): 427.

not lose out to Rotterdam in the short run. However, it is perhaps too early to tell how the situation will develop in the years to come.

*In the European Communities (*ECSC *and* EEC*)*
So far, strictly national and regional attitudes to the project have been discussed, and this might seem surprising in view of the fact that the last two decades have been characterized by efforts towards European economic unity. It had been one of the aims of the coal and steel pool to "contribute ... to economic expansion, growth of employment, and raising of the standard of living in the member States" (Article 2 of the ECSC Treaty). But we have seen that the ECSC High Authority (and later the EEC Commission) were given very limited powers in the field of transport policy; yet this field should be an essential component of a common economic policy. Given this situation, the attitude of the European organizations has been one of "wait and see," although some recommendations were made to member states concerning a common transport infrastructure.[34]

For example, one of the most important recommendations of the EEC Commission with respect to inland waterways concerned the Rhône-Rhine links via the Moselle and Doubs valleys (see Figure 2). The Commission believed that "the creation of the great North-South axis would allow the maritime ports to be linked with their natural hinterlands and would provide a direct outlet for the Rhineland's industry to the Mediterranean." The project of a north-south river axis dates back to the Romans. The work of ECMT in the field of transport infrastructure has been far more constructive: it was seen that in addition to advocating standardized European networks (and the EEC Commission's recommendations were basically taken from ECMT resolutions in this respect), the ECMT studied and recommended standard barge designs and the extensive use, where economically feasible, of such modern techniques as the elevator-lock, the use of radar in navigation, and the transport of bulky materials in 3200-ton pushed convoys of one tugboat and two or more "dumb" barges.

It is indeed ironic (and perhaps reflects the fragile nature of the European economic and technical cooperation achieved so far) that supposedly supranational organizations (ECSC, EEC) have had much less success in achieving concrete results than a mere Conference of Transport Ministers of 18 sovereign states whose resolutions are not any easier to enforce than UN General Assembly resolutions! When and how a greater degree of cooperation in European transport policy will be achieved is open to speculation, but in any case this seems to be one of the major stumbling blocks in the path of the continent's economic integration.

34 CEE, Commission, *Recommandations de la Commission en vue du développement de l'infrastructure dans le cadre de la Communauté* (Brussels: CEE, 1960-61). (Mimeographed).

Since European cooperation still left much to be desired, the canalization of the Moselle was finally accepted by the three countries concerned only after 10 years of fighting, discussing, bickering, and negotiating in the tradition of old-fashioned bilateral diplomacy. But in spite of a weak institutional framework, the "European idea" did help psychologically, for without its presence it is doubtful whether the Germans would have endorsed the project, hostile as they generally were to an undertaking which they have always considered contrary to their interests.

Even though canalization was not achieved within the framework of a strongly united Europe, its repercussions on the evolution of the European economy should not be underestimated. This aspect will be referred to with more emphasis in the conclusion, but two remarks should be made in this connection before the project itself can be discussed in some detail. First, the canalization of the Moselle, inasmuch as it favors Lorraine more than the Ruhr, might tend to strengthen a European Community far too powerfully dominated by the West German economy. Secondly, the endless internal struggles between European States have been a key factor in the continent's political and economic decline, because they have tied down enormous amounts of manpower, energy, and resources (natural and financial) in non-productive pursuits. For Europe to regain at least some of its past economic power, the key sectors of the European economy must be entrusted to the supranational authorities which already exist and function as embryos of a future confederation. This includes transportation, and such projects as the canalization of the Moselle can only be worthwhile in the long run if they are carried out and administered on a supranational basis. Finally, the project can only be judged acceptable when the countries concerned realize that their economies, largely oriented in an east-west direction within their respective boundaries, can once again be re-oriented in the traditional (pre-1700) north-south axis of trade and interregional linkages. Michel summarized the role of the new Moselle waterway in the conclusion of his article in the following terms: "It has taken three major wars and a fundamental shift in the continental balance of power to reorient economic thinking to the north-south axis. ... ECSC and EEC represent the political and economic expressions of the revival of the north-south orientation, including the Rhine axis and its Moselle branch."[35]

This political and economic situation of the past thirty years is, of course, a direct result of the post-war ideological division of Europe. Initially, and for many years, western and eastern Europe engaged in mutually exclusive paths of economic cooperation and integration. But it is by no means certain that this cleavage will remain as absolute as in the early years of the "cold war." On the

35 Aloys A. Michel, "The Canalization of the Moselle and West European Integration," *Geographical Review* 52, no. 4 (1962): 491.

contrary, there are many indications that an east-west dialogue has now begun and progressed to the point where trade has resumed across the once tight "Iron Curtain." Increased trade will necessarily mean a more intensive utilization of major east-west routes such as the Danube and the Mittelland Canal. Only as part of such a complete waterways network can the Moselle become the truly European route its promoters want it to become. In the words of two high officials of the Société Internationale de la Moselle: "... the canalization of the Moselle from Koblenz to Thionville is of course only a step within the achievement of a much vaster enterprise which will allow some day for Rhine craft to reach the Mediterranean shores to the south as well as the Black Sea to the east."[36]

Of course, it is quite obvious that the trans-European east-west link is still at best a long-range project, even though its partial implementation has already begun: the Rhine-Main-Danube link is almost completed, the Meuse-Rhine Canal between Maastricht and Düsseldorf is one of the 12 links recommended by the ECMT and might be built in the near future; and it is possible that the French government might increase the draft, width, and headroom on the Marne-Rhine Canal, thus establishing a deep-draft link between Strasbourg and the already canalized Seine River. Finally, provided that the relations between the German Federal Republic and East Germany continue to improve, the Mittelland Canal might be deepened and widened, as could be the case for the Brandenburg Canal, the Elbe, the Oder (which through Czechoslovakia's Morava River will some day be linked to the Danube near Bratislava). But apart from the first one, nothing has yet been decided with respect to these links. Many of these imply a much greater degree of east-west cooperation than the European governments have been willing to accept since the events of 1968 in Prague. At any rate, the canalized Moselle could presumably serve as a convenient route for the export of French steel products to eastern European countries (especially Yugoslavia, Rumania, and Poland), since there is no apparent reason why those countries could not increase their commercial ties with the West. This will be all the more attractive since the Iron Gates section of the Danube is currently being improved for use by the largest existing barges.

In the near future, north-south inland waterway links in western Europe seem to stand a much better chance of being improved. In the first place, Paris is now linked with the deep-draft Belgian system through the improvement of the Scheldt and the recent completion of the Canal du Nord. Secondly, there is a very good chance that the French section of the Meuse will also be improved in the near future, either through canalization of the river itself or by enlarging the capacity of the Canal de l'Est (northern branch). Thirdly, current work on the

---

36 Augustin Jordan and Rolf Lahr, "Signification historique et européene de la canalisation de la Moselle" (French/German), *L'aménagement de la Moselle* (Trier: SIM, 1966), p. 32.

upper Moselle (between Metz and Neuves-Maisons; see Figure 2) and on the Toul-Nancy section of the Marne-Rhine Canal is but the first stage of an ambitious plan to link the Moselle and Saône with a deep-draft canal. After years of debate and hesitation, the French government, early in 1967, decided to ask the European Investment Bank (a specialized agency of the EEC) to finance the work to be carried out between Neuves-Maisons and Chalon-sur-Saône since it had been classified (by the ECMT in 1953 and by the EEC Commission in 1960) as of interest to Europe as a whole. The French are also enlarging the Rhône-Rhine Canal and building new port facilities along it. Probably the north-south project which has the least chance to succeed is the Transhelvetic Canal (Rhône-Lake Geneva-Lake Neuchâtel-Aar River-Rhine) because it would be too expensive to carry out and not at all competitive with the Meuse, Saône-Moselle, and Rhône-Rhine routes through northeastern France. All these projects will be discussed later in connection with traffic and prospects for regional development along existing and planned waterways. But the administrative, technical, and economic aspects of the final Moselle project must first be examined.

VI
The Canalized Moselle River
(1956-1973)

One would do a great injustice to the project by trying to discuss it only as a motive for conflicting human attitudes. But without such a discussion, the project would be of little interest to all but a few civil engineers and others directly concerned by it. However, once the background is known, some attention should be given to the project itself. To divide it up into various "aspects" is arbitrary but done for the sake of clarity and with the understanding that any one "aspect" is only part of an interrelated complex which cannot be fully understood without some knowledge of its component parts – technical, economic, administrative, and financial.

The Moselle rises at Bussang Pass in the southern Vosges Mountains at an elevation of 735 m, and reaches its confluence with the Rhine at Koblenz at an elevation of 59 m. Its total length is 520 km, of which 278 km is in France, 36 km between Luxembourg and West Germany, and 206 km is in West Germany. Its drainage basin (Figure 4) covers some 28,000 square km in the Vosges, Ardennes, Hunsrück, and Eifel mountains. The Moselle has great variations in stream discharge due to the very marked seasonality of its water supply. Downstream from the Saar-Moselle confluence, the discharge of the Moselle ranges from 18 cubic meters per second to 4000 cubic meters per second, reflecting the summertime low-water mark in the former case, and the early spring floods fed by heavy rainfall and snowmelt in the Vosges Mountains in the latter. The difference between the two extreme levels may be as great as 10 meters on the

German Moselle. The average slope of the river between Thionville and Koblenz is 1/3000 or 33 cm/km (Figure 5).[1]

The technical aspect of the project is the least controversial because technology is by definition international: barring certain inhibiting factors (physical, cultural, or political), knowledge of certain techniques spreads without difficulty across national boundaries. It is much easier for two or three nations to agree upon the design of a lock than upon the economic benefits to be derived from the use of the lock under construction. This brings up the whole question of the transport route as a state-supported non-profit undertaking or as a private profit-making venture. In the latter case, few large-scale projects could ever be built because with heavy initial capital outlays it is very difficult to break even in the short run and no profits can be expected for a number of years (the case of the St Lawrence Seaway is a good example of this), even though the transport route is operating at full capacity. Therefore, most states agree to the need for public investment in such projects. But some states introduce the profit-making factor into the picture when they feel that their national interest is threatened by the implementation of the project. In this case, they put forth extreme financial estimates which would make the project essentially uneconomical, while basically agreeing with the proposed technical, administrative, and legal framework of the project.

This abstract situation applies exactly to the case of the Moselle. In the technical aspects only was the agreement between the French and the Germans almost complete. Differences were greater in the administrative and legal aspects, but not insurmountable. The real conflict of interests arose at the economic and financial level, and this on the very eve of the signature of the 1956 convention. Ironically, the Germans, who had violently opposed the project in the early 1950s, had actually initiated it in 1941 (Staat-Leblanc project; see chapter v) by beginning the construction of the Koblenz dam. But their project did not allow for a sufficient draft for Rhine barges and implied the construction of new craft, which would add to the expense of the canalization proper. Moreover, a free-flowing improved river channel between Trier and Koblenz did not solve the basic problems of floods and low water. Finally, very little was made of the considerable potential hydro-electric power which could be generated by a series of low dams. In 1947, René Malcor, Director of Public Works and Transport Authority of the Land of Rheinland-Pfalz, then under French military administration, took up the 1941 project and ordered work resumed on the Koblenz dam. The latter was completed in 1951 and included four 4000-kw electric generators, the first of which was put into service at the same time as the dam was completed.[2]

1 Charles Chevrier and Hans Bormann, "Les travaux d'aménagement de la Moselle" (French/German), *L'aménagement de la Moselle* (Trier: SIM, 1966), pp. 50-1.
2 *RNIR* **23**, no. 3 (1951): 93; and *L'Usine Nouvelle* (25 January 1951).

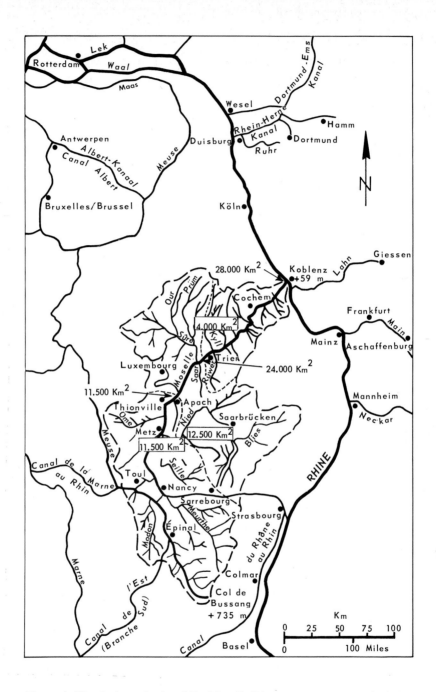

Figure 4 The drainage basin of the Moselle River.

118

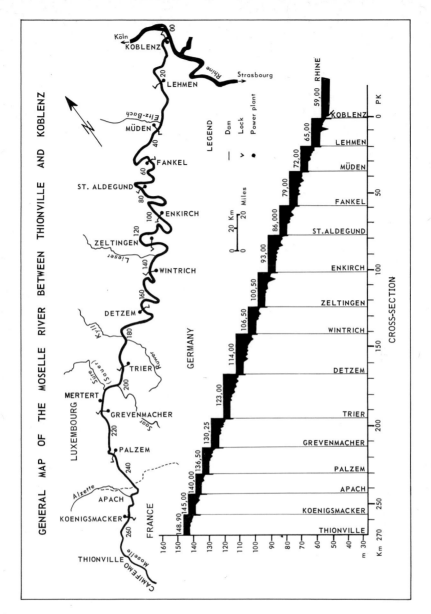

Figure 5 Map and cross-section of the canalized Moselle River between Thionville and Koblenz.

119

But Malcor was not satisfied with the Staat-Leblanc project as it was. In the period of shortages immediately following the war, he realized that neither funds nor equipment were available for a large-scale project. However in September 1949, at the 17th International Navigation Congress held in Lisbon, Malcor recognized that "there are no shortages any longer and since the chief problem becomes that of financing [the project], the canalization [alternative] becomes attractive due to the production of electric power."[3]

Unfortunately for the French promoters of the project, this statement added fuel to the fire, because it implied that the profits made on the sale of electric power produced on the Moselle would be sufficient to cover the added cost of canalizing the whole Thionville-Koblenz section (instead of just the Thionville-Trier section). Later studies and other documentary evidence point to the fact that the Germans did not miss an opportunity to use such an argument, hoping that this would automatically ruin any chance of an economically viable project. This aspect of the question is discussed under the financial aspects of the project; it illustrates the argument above concerning the means to pay for large-scale infrastructure works. But this apparently unrelated problem helped determine the final manner in which the technical aspects of the project would be handled.

Malcor's 1949 recommendations in Lisbon were followed by a surge of interest in solving the technical problems on the part of all three national public works administrations concerned, although those in France and Luxembourg had already written their reports (Germany was still under Allied military occupation, so that Malcor's 1949 report was used for the German section of the river). Beginning in January 1952, when West Germany had regained sovereign status, the Baden-Baden meeting and other international reunions settled the technical question to a large extent, although the 1955-56 Franco-German Commission's report was the final basis of the convention articles relating to technical questions.[4]

The section of the 1956 report dealing with technical aspects of the project made a distinction between infrastructure and electric power. Under the former

---

3 René Malcor, "Rapport sur la canalisation de la Moselle," *Comptes-Rendus du XVIIe Congrès International de la Navigation*, Lisbon (September 1949): 5.

4 France, Ministère des Affaires Etrangères, *Rapport de la Commission franco-allemande pour l'étude de la canalisation de la Moselle* (Paris: Imprimerie Nationale, 1956); and "Convention du 27 octobre 1956 entre la République Française, la République Fédérale d'Allemagne, et le Grand-Duché de Luxembourg au sujet de la canalisation de la Moselle," *Journal Officiel* (France), 10 January 1957, *Bundesgesetzblatt* (West Germany), 24 December 1956, and *Mémorial* (Luxembourg), 29 December 1956, Chapter I, Article 1, and Appendix 1: "Description des travaux faisant l'objet de la Convention" (all texts in French or German).

heading, the report recommended improving the river channel for navigation by 1350-1500-ton barges between Thionville and Koblenz, a river distance of 270 km; the new waterway was to use the river channel except for two 1-km-long side canals. In addition to the dam in Koblenz, 13 others were to be built (9 in West Germany, 1 on the German-Luxembourg border, and 3 in France), all but the French ones including power plants. The total cost of the project (including the power plants) was estimated at 517.9 million DM ($130 million) at 1955 prices, to which the German experts added 120 million DM ($30 million) for building a second lock along each dam and for extending the construction period from 5 to 7 years (2 years for preliminary studies and 5 for construction). Under the heading of electric power, it was estimated that the total yearly output of the Moselle plants would be 747 million kwh, of which 689 million would be marketable. The power would be sold at 3.5 pfennigs (about 85/100 cent US) per kwh if the operation of the plants and power distribution were handled by the same firm.

There was such a degree of consensus on technical matters that the appendix to the 1956 Convention dealing with the work to be carried out restated almost word for word the Commission's recommendations, including the number of dams and power plants, ports, locks, waiting spaces for barges, fish scales, administration buildings, sizes of locks and other dimensions, signalling equipment for night-time navigation, and "the measures necessary to avoid damages resulting from the works, unless they have been compensated for." But the convention's text was less specific on the question of power plants. The type of works carried out could be divided into 6 major categories:

1 the 13 dams to be built, including the power plants and adjoining locks (one lock was added to the Koblenz dam);

2 dredging and removal of rocks from the riverbed in order to guarantee a minimum navigation draft and width of channel;

3 the building of 4 shelter ports (Senheim, Bernkastel-Kues, Trier, and Koenigsmacker);

4 the raising of some bridges and consolidation of their substructure;

5 the provision of all necessary auxiliary equipment for the sake of safe navigation, e.g., channel markers, lighting of lock facilities and of barge waiting areas, light signals, loudspeakers at lock sites, telephone and radio facilities, and kilometer markers along the waterway;

6 all measures designed to prevent damages resulting from the canalization works, such as the rerouting of sewers, water mains, and tributary stream mouths, the protection of some groups of dwellings or the waterproofing of some isolated houses, the raising of riverbank roads and tow-paths, the modernization of ferry operations, and the protection of riparian cultivated fields through the construction of retaining walls over a height of one meter above the new

Plate 8 The Koenigsmacker lock on the French section of the canalized Moselle River. Author's photograph, 21 April 1965.

water level. As will be seen under the financial aspects of the project, all these improvements were the main cause for the total cost exceeding by far the 1956 estimates.

The canalization proper was a fairly simple and inexpensive project from the technical standpoint. It consisted in a step-like division of the river into 14 "ponds" (*biefs*) by means of an equal number of dams (see Figure 5). The length of each pond varies from 11 to 29 km, the average length being 19.2 km. The navigable prism is 40 m wide at the surface on straight sections and wider in the meanders or curves, and 2.90 m deep. The height of the dams varies from 3.90 to 9 m, the average being 6.40 m. With each dam there is one navigation lock for barges (length: 170 m, width: 12 m, and depth: 3.50 m), with room for a second parallel lock of equal dimensions, and one for pleasure craft (length: 18 m, width: 3.50 m, and depth: 1.50 m); some of the dams are also provided with passages for canoes. All installations are built according to a standard design, even though a large number of contractors and sub-contractors were at work. The project took seven years to build (March 1958 to January 1964) but was not inaugurated by the three chiefs of state until 26 May 1964, and was not opened to navigation until 1 June 1964. After that date, some work still went

122

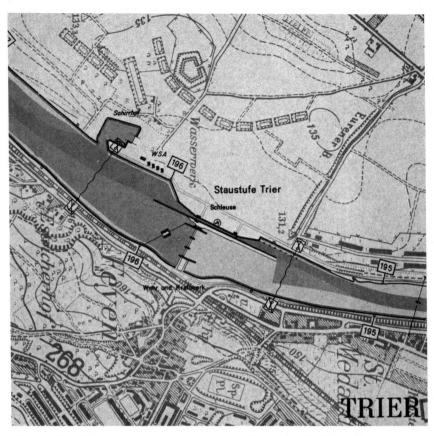

Plate 9 The Trier dam and lock on the canalized Moselle River (base map scale 1:10,000). Source: *Die Mosel von Thionville bis Koblenz: Schiffahrstskarte* (1964), Sheet No. 12 (Trier). (Boatmen's atlas, with legends in German and French.)

on, but it was essentially one of completing the landscaping and taking care of minor technical details.[5]

However interesting the technical aspects of the project may have been, they by no means reflected the application of new technology, since other waterways (St Lawrence, Volga, Neckar, Main, Rhône) had been improved with identical methods. Therefore, no difficulties were encountered during the construction,

5 Chevrier and Bormann, *L'aménagement de la Moselle*, pp. 50-80; and Ferdinand Kinnen, "La construction du port de Mertert," *Le port de Mertert et la navigation de la Moselle* (Luxembourg: Société du Port Fluvial de Mertert, 1966), pp. 51-80.

save for occasional frosts and flooding. But the economic, administrative, and financial problems were far more complex.

The economic aspects of the project included transport costs, tolls, volume of traffic estimates, and economic repercussions of the new waterway. The French and German experts disagreed on all these questions. While the French logically assumed that the freight rates on the new waterway should be about equal to those on the Rhine and its other major tributaries, the Germans believed that Moselle rates should be about 25 per cent higher. Moreover, in order to prove that the project would be uneconomical, the Germans stood on the principle that the tolls to be charged should cover all capital investments in the project (excluding the power plants), and also all the operation, maintenance, and renewal costs. This gave a German toll rate estimate ranging from 3.90 DM ($0.95) to 8.75 DM ($2.20) per ton, with annual traffic hypotheses of 9 and 4 million tons respectively.

The French argued that this principle had never been applied in any inland waterways policy, otherwise recent West German projects (Main, Neckar) could never even have been started. They also noted that on most major European waterways (Rhine, Elbe, Danube, Seine, Rhône, Meuse) no tolls were being charged; but since moderate tolls were being charged on the Neckar and Main, those on the Moselle should be equivalent, i.e., about 50 pfennigs ($0.12) per ton between Thionville and Koblenz, a figure very much lower than German toll rate estimates. Accordingly, the French concluded that total transport costs (including tolls) on the canalized Moselle would be much cheaper for most products than via the traditional transport routes (rail or mixed rail-water route via the Rhine and Strasbourg). For example, the transport of a ton of coking coal from the Ruhr to Rombas (Lorraine) by rail cost 1900 FF (old francs) in 1955 ($5.43); through the Moselle, the cost would be reduced to 1212 FF ($3.46); for steel shipped from Rombas to Antwerp, the cost would drop from 2078 FF per ton by rail ($5.95) or from 1609 FF via Strasbourg and the Rhine ($4.60) to 820 FF via the new waterway ($2.34).[6] Such low costs would lead to a very heavy volume of traffic – almost 5 million tons for the first year of full operation in each direction, without taking into account long-term economic fluctuations.

Traffic estimates will be discussed later on in connection with the actual operation and prospects of the new waterway. Suffice it to say that the Germans did not believe in the possibility of any kind of traffic on the canalized Moselle, arguing that rail transport would always be cheaper, given their assumed level of freight and toll rates on the new waterway. But for the sake of discussing its economic repercussions, they agreed to consider the French traffic hypothesis as valid, in obvious contradiction to their own assumptions. They argued that the

6 France, *Commission franco-allemande*, pp. 172-3.

project would have catastrophic consequences on the West German economy due to a transport cost saving of 7 billion FF ($20 million) for the French; this would favor the French economy alone and cause heavy losses to the Bundesbahn. One fails to see anything but the most narrow-minded national self-interest in such a line of reasoning. The French argued that existing means of transport did not have exclusive traffic rights when the Lorraine heavy industry was in such an inferior competitive position vis-à-vis the Ruhr and other European industrial regions for lack of adequate transportation. However, the new waterway would benefit some sectors of the West German economy.

On economic questions, the Moselle Convention was essentially a compromise. Tolls were established, but they would be no higher than those charged on the Neckar and Main. Lock facilities were provided for an estimated annual traffic of 10 million tons, but except at Koblenz, no second locks were built although space was provided alongside each existing lock for the eventual addition of a new one. Finally, too, revenues were essentially earmarked for administrative expenses first, but also for capital investment and interests, although it was realized that the total cost of the project could not be paid easily or entirely from this source, as the Germans would have liked.

Administrative and legal aspects included the problems of whether the project should be built and operated by one or two authorities, what the nationality and functions of these should be, and how should freedom of navigation be enforced. Both sides agreed that the physical unity of the river called for the creation of a single authority for the implementation of the project. The French wanted to entrust both canalization and power plant works to a single corporation, while the Germans wanted one company for the canalization works and another one for the power plant works. The latter would then be carried out by Rheinische-Westfalisches Elektrizitätswerk A.G. (RWE). Again, the solution to these differences was one of compromise: Article 7 of the Moselle Convention states that "the construction of the power plants and utilization of the hydroelectric energy of the Moselle are reserved for each of the Contracting States on its territory."[7] This meant that the Germans had won their argument; on the other hand, none of the income from the power plants would be used to pay for the canalization works, as the Germans had wanted; the dam and power plant would be built independently from each other, but if both dam and power plant were built by the same contractor, costs would be split equitably so that international financing would pay for lock and dam only. The two plants at Grevenmacher and Palzem on the German-Luxembourg section of the Moselle were

7 Alfred Giuliani, "Les centrales hydro-électriques de la Moselle," *Le port de Mertert et la navigation de la Moselle* (Luxembourg: Société du Port Fluvial de Mertert, 1966), pp. 89-156; and Gerhard Lenssen, "Die Ausnutzung der Wasserkräfte der ausgebauten Mosel", *L'aménagement de la Moselle* (Trier: SIM 1966), pp. 243-8.

built and operated by the Luxembourg private power company, Société Electrique de l'Our, which would sell half of the power to West Germany. The French dams included no power plants for lack of sufficiently high waterfalls. This may explain the weakness of the French bargaining position on this point.

As for the canalization works proper, both sides agreed to the establishment of a publicly sponsored joint-stock company incorporated in one of the three riparian States. For both geographical and historical reasons, this company, the Société Internationale de la Moselle or Internationale Mosel-Gesellschaft (hereafter referred to as SIM), was established as a German corporation with headquarters in Trier. Even though the internal structure of the SIM need not be described in detail, it is interesting to note its deliberately well-balanced composition: there are two German and two French managers (gérants), and the Board of Directors (Conseil de Surveillance) is made up of 6 Germans, 6 Frenchmen, and 2 Luxemburgers. Likewise, the SIM's capital is made up of 50 million DM ($12.5 million) contributed by West Germany, 50 million by France, and 2 million ($0.5 million) by Luxembourg, divided into equal shares of 10,000 DM ($2,500) each. Article 3 of the SIM's Statutes (Appendix 2 of the 1956 Convention) states that "the company's aim is to finance and carry out, with the cooperation of the national navigation authorities, the improvement of the Moselle between Thionville and Koblenz for 1500-ton barge traffic" in accordance with the provisions of the convention. But beginning 1 June 1964, the national administrations have taken over the operation, maintenance, and renewal of the installations, while "the company continues for its part to assume the cost of the remaining work, of closing the bids, and of carrying out all the eventual measures of protection against flood damage."[8]

While the SIM's role was by definition temporary, the three riparian States did agree upon a limited degree of inter-governmental cooperation when they decided to establish the Moselle Commission (Articles 39-44 of the 1956 Convention). This Commission is made up of 6 members, 2 from each riparian State. It began to function in Trier on 21 December 1962. Its aim is "to insure the maintenance of the highest degree of prosperity for navigation on the Moselle" (Article 40), but its powers are much more limited than those of the Central Rhine Commission, although it is responsible for setting and collecting tolls. Freedom of navigation applies to the river between Koblenz and Metz in both directions and for craft of all nations. Regardless of nationality, all barges are free to use public ports and their installations without restrictions. Navigation on the Moselle is subject to the free navigation clauses of the Mannhaim act of 1868 as revised in 1919 and 1945, although this freedom is partially restricted

8 Société Internationale de la Moselle (G.m.b.H.), *Geschäftsbericht/Rapport de Gestion: 1965* (German/French) (Trier: SIM, 1966), p. 4.

because of tolls, which are designed to finance in part the canalization project. Concerning financing, the Convention gave satisfaction to the Germans when it took the power plants out of the canalization project proper. Since West Germany and Luxembourg had already paid for the plants, France had to pay for two-thirds of the construction costs proper. Most of the necessary funds were raised by the SIM through international loans guaranteed by the French and West German governments. Primarily because of price increases since 1955, the need to adapt the new waterway to navigation by pushed barges, and the enormous cost of riverbank protection and land expropriation, the early cost estimates were underestimated by over one-half of the total cost. It finally amounted to 780 million DM ($195 million), including 292.2 million for dredging operations, 267.2 million for locks and dams, 102.4 million for riverbank protection, 65 million for administrative expenses, 33.1 million for land expropriation and indemnization, 5.1 million for preliminary work, 3.1 million for buildings, and 11.6 million for other works (Table 16). With all the problems, difficulties, and disagreements, the Moselle canalization project was comparatively inexpensive, because it was technically simple to build and economical to operate. How successful it has been (and could become) in fulfilling its threefold function is the object of the remaining discussion.

EARLY RESULTS: 1964-1973

The major problem in evaluating early results for such a project as the canalized Moselle is the lack of historical perspective. It is easy to claim that the success of the new waterway has been spectacular. But such a claim must be qualified: in the first place, progress is measured in relation to a traffic which was non-existent before 1 June 1964, or to one which took place on antiquated canals which were too shallow, too narrow, obstructed with too many locks, and had too little headroom for the requirements of a modern industrial economy. Secondly, the volume of traffic during the first full year of operation was far below expectations, although this should not be surprising in the light of past experience on such improved waterways as the St Lawrence Seaway. Finally, there is relatively little diversification in the traffic pattern because it takes a period of adjustment for manufacturers or other users of transport means to change over from rail to water transport. There is also little doubt that rail transport is more economical for certain goods (mostly high-value and low-weight), but there is a lack of statistical data to back up this assumption. Moreover, how much rail traffic has been captured by the waterway should also be known before any judgment can be made, but such information is also very difficult to obtain. A final reservation must be made in any meaningful traffic evaluation, namely that such unknowns as the change-over to new or supplemental

127

energy sources and increasing imports of iron ore from overseas might drastically affect current patterns of volume and the nature of goods carried by the various modes of transport.

Before the actual traffic patterns can be discussed, it would be worthwhile to describe the 1956 Franco-German Commission's estimates of traffic on the canalized Moselle during the first full year of operation (Table 8). The attitude of the German delegation and its argument was discussed earlier. On that basis, it is not surprising that the Germans estimated total upbound traffic at less than 200,000 tons, given existing railroad rates and toll levels based upon a total potential traffic of 9 million tons in both directions. For downbound traffic, however, they did concede the possibility of 1,249,000 tons under the same conditions, over 1 million of which would be made up of pig-iron and steel exports from Lorraine. To the less than 1.5 million ton figure advanced by the Germans, the French responded with a total of nearly 10 million tons, with upbound traffic only slightly more important in volume, excluding all traffic to and from Luxembourg. Of the 4.7 million tons shipped upstream, 2.5 million tons were coke sent to northern Lorraine mostly from the Ruhr. Coking coal shipped to Lorraine steel mills and coke furnaces, mostly from the Ruhr and the US, accounted for another 1.3 million tons, while high-grade iron ore and manganese ore, both shipped to Lorraine from overseas, would total 450,000 tons. In downbound traffic (estimated at 4,250,000 tons), the largest share was held by pig-iron and steel exported from Lorraine and the Saar (1.6 million tons, 22 per cent of which came from the Saar), but finished metal products accounted for 250,000 tons, with identical volumes for cement and blast-furnace slag exports. Coal exports from Lorraine and the Saar would amount to 400,000 and 300,000 tons respectively. In addition to these shipments to and from Moselle ports, traffic to and from the Trier-Koblenz section of the river was estimated at 1 million tons. One obvious item is missing from this list: iron ore exports to the Ruhr. The French noted the past importance of these and envisaged an annual traffic of 2.4 million tons, but the Germans declared that they were not interested in resuming this trade, so that the item was dropped from the French estimates. This was in obvious accordance with West German national self-interest (which made high-grade Swedish ore more attractive) and against the spirit of European cooperation within the ECSC framework; but perhaps this was a small price to pay for the fact that Germany had finally agreed to the principle of canalizing the Moselle River — though, as we have seen, by no means without compensations.

These traffic forecasts were of course based on very different assumptions as to the evolution of freight rates in the near future. The German experts foresaw a steep increase in navigation rates, while the French experts believed that excellent physical conditions on the Moselle would tend to bring them down. On the other hand, the Germans believed in a sharp decline in railroad freight rates while the French thought they would go up. In fact, both were right in part. The German experts were right in that rail transport costs for steel products between Lorraine and the North Sea ports went down; the same happened to freight rates applied to coke transport between the Ruhr and Thionville, which suddenly dropped 35 to 40 per cent when the new waterway was opened: thus, transport of a ton of coke cost 13 DM ($3.25) in 1965 as compared to 23.80 DM ($6) in 1955.[9] On the other hand, the French experts had been right about the drop in river and canal rates, including the Moselle: the combined transport cost of a ton of coke from the Ruhr to Thionville (12 DM or $3) and of a ton of steel products from Thionville to Antwerp (11 DM or $2.75) – two commodities linked by virtue of return cargo arrangements – amounted to 23 DM ($5.75) in 1965 (including tolls) as compared to 43.30 DM ($11) via Strasbourg and the Rhine in 1955.[10]

But while the French experts' forecasts concerning freight rates proved to be essentially correct, their traffic predictions were much higher than the reality. Various reasons could be given for this situation: the return of the Saar to Germany in 1959 reoriented the Saar's transport interests away from the Moselle and towards the construction of a Saar-Pfalz-Rhein Canal to Mannheim, whose potential benefits are being compensated by the Als-ob-Tarife. The transport infrastructure in Lorraine, especially the Moselle south of Metz, the Marne-Rhine Canal, and the Canal de l'Est (southern branch) have not yet been improved to accommodate deep-draft barges; thus, the canalized Moselle is still nothing but a heavily-travelled cul-de-sac. River port facilities on the Moselle are still inadequate. The catalyzing effect of the new waterway as a prime agent in regional development is far slower than many would believe. And probably the major reason for slow development of traffic on the Moselle is that drastic railroad rate cuts have tried to make up for cheaper water transport costs resulting in traffic captures for several important commodities.

Even so, in 1965, the first full calendar year of navigation on the canalized Moselle, total traffic through the Apach lock at the Franco-German border amounted to 3,210,808 tons in both directions, upstream and downstream movement being about equal in volume. This total exceeded 4 million tons in 1966, 6.5 million in 1969, and 7.6 million in 1973. In 1965, total traffic at the Koblenz locks totalled 4,598,000 tons, of which about 60 per cent consisted of

9 This was due to the introduction by the railways of low, so-called "Als-ob" rates, meaning "as if" the traffic went by water.

10 Jean Aubathier, "La Moselle après son ouverture à la grande navigation" (French/German), *L'aménagement de la Moselle* (Trier: SIM, 1966), pp. 296-8. In this excellent article, the author describes and evaluates all aspects of navigation on the Moselle during the first two years of operation.

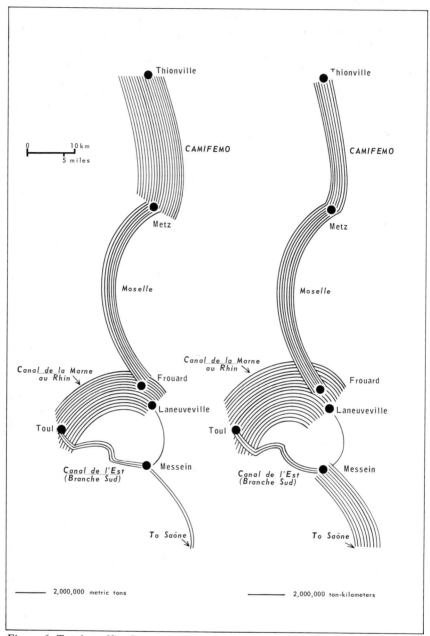

Figure 6 Total traffic flows on the French Moselle, 1965 (in tons and ton-kilometers). (Source: Table 6.) *Note:* this figure cannot be updated due to lack of comparable post-1965 data.

upbound traffic. Traffic at Koblenz totalled some 5.8 million tons in 1966, 9.4 million in 1969, and 10.6 million in 1973.[11] The upward trend of monthly traffic volumes over the initial two-year period (Figures 9 and 10) indicates that the promoters of the project had every reason to feel optimistic. Traffic expansion has taken place in a spectacular fashion, although one must again emphasize past experience on other waterways in that the growth of traffic is bound to be slow and not to live up to its promoters' expectations for at least several years. On the other hand, some traffic, such as that to and from the port of Mertert (Luxembourg), had been left aside in the 1956 forecasts but has proven to be quite successful in its growth and volumes of shipments and receipts: from 370,000 tons in 1966, traffic at Mertert has risen to 943,000 tons in 1967, to 1,130,000 tons in 1968, and to 1,435,000 tons in 1973. In any case, comparative studies could throw more light on the problems of traffic growth in deep-draft inland navigation.

More specifically, upbound traffic on the Moselle is mostly made up of solid mineral fuels. In addition to the very low railroad rates, which have allowed the railroads to retain their monopoly in supplying coke to the Longwy, Saar, Pont-à-Mousson, Pompey, and Neuves-Maisons steel plants, progress in steel-making techniques have reduced the percentage of coke needed to make a ton of steel. The combination of these two factors helps to explain a 1965 volume of 1,410,010 tons of upbound fuels (coal, coke, etc.) as compared to 1956 estimates of about 4 million tons (2,658,988 tons in 1973). For example, at the Apach border crossing in 1965, some 2 million tons of coke entered France by rail, by comparison with only 750,000 tons on the Moselle. Some American and German coal imported by Lorraine also came by way of the Meuse, Strasbourg, and the Marne-Rhine Canal, thus avoiding the new waterway. Other categories of products fall far behind: steel products (48,000 tons in 1965, 226,000 tons in 1973), sulphur (40,000 tons in 1965, 65,000 tons in 1973), and iron and manganese ores (18,000 tons in 1965, 280,000 tons in 1966, and 760,000 tons in 1973). The latter increase is the most spectacular and in some respects most significant of the current trends in West European steel-making.

For reasons similar to those stated in the case of upbound traffic, downbound traffic did not expand as much as expected. Steel products, by far the largest category (1.1 million tons in 1965, same volume in 1973) represent (almost

11 *RNIR* **36**, no. 13 (1964), through **46**, no. 11 (1974). This journal (which changed its name to *Revue de la Navigation Fluviale Européenne* in 1969) is the best single source for detailed (monthly) traffic data on the canalized Moselle River. Unfortunately, my total for these data do not always coincide with the *RNIR*'s totals, even after patient double-checking. Moreover, beginning in June 1965, port and nature of goods data are not as detailed and not strictly comparable; notably lacking are detailed West German port statistics, because those figures published during the first year had been used by the Bundesbahn to establish special freight rates along similar routes.

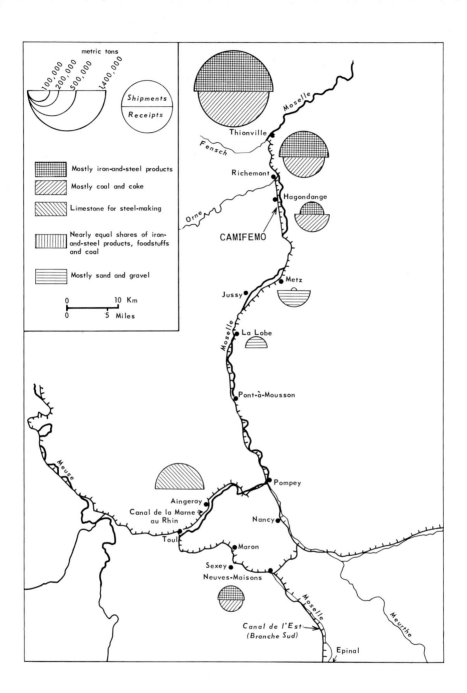

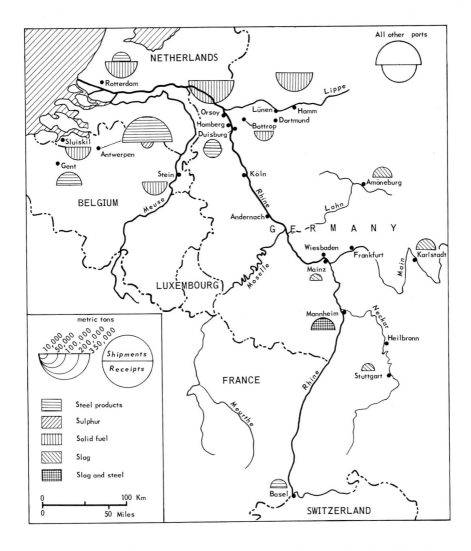

Figure 7 (left) Traffic of the main ports on the French Moselle, 1965. Shipments and receipts. Indicates only those ports handling over 100,000 tons a year. (Source: Table 7.) *Note:* this map cannot be updated due to lack of comparable post-1965 data.

Figure 8 (above) Traffic on the canalized Moselle to and from French ports, June 1964 to May 1965, indicating major ports of origin and destination outside France. (Source: Tables 12 and 13.)

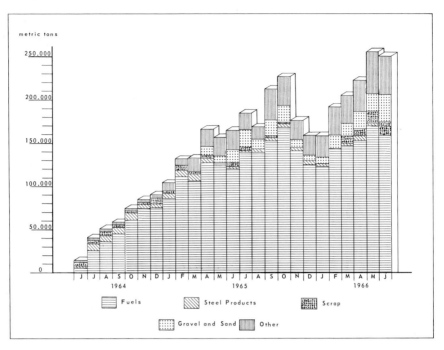

Figure 9 Monthly evolution of upbound traffic on the canalized Moselle, June 1964 to June 1966. This graph cannot be updated due to lack of comparable post-1966 data.

exclusively) shipments out of the area north of Metz, shipments from the Longwy and Nancy areas being exported almost entirely by rail. The second category, granulated blast-furnace slag for West German cement plants, surpassed the experts' forecast by far (440,000 tons in 1965 – over 8 times the estimated amount – and 939,000 tons in 1973). This is accounted for by the much cheaper transport costs which made such traffic economical. All other downbound items were shipped in very small volumes. In 1965 and 1966, Luxembourg and German traffic was not yet well developed because of delays in building the adequate port facilities at Trier and Mertert, completed respectively in May 1965 and September 1966. Since 1966, Luxembourg and German traffic has picked up substantially, as was seen in the case of Mertert. Table 11 indicates that the traffic at the Koblenz locks is predominantly bound for or coming from France, which accounts for about two-thirds of the total. Luxembourg accounts for about 13 per cent, the Koblenz pond for about 9 per cent and the other German Moselle ports, mostly Trier, for another 10 per cent in 1973. (In 1965, Luxembourg was not yet involved in Moselle traffic, so that French and German traffic accounted for 71 and 26 per cent of the total respectively.)

134

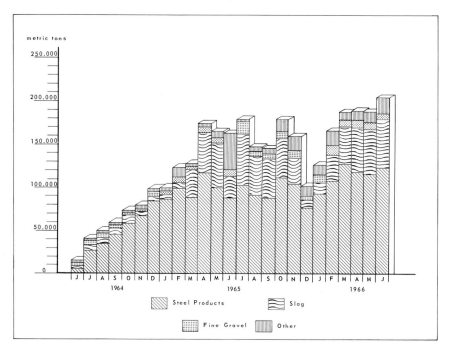

Figure 10 Monthly evolution of downbound traffic on the canalized Moselle, June 1964 to June 1966. This graph cannot be updated due to lack of comparable post-1966 data.

Finally, the compilation of port statistics for the period June 1964-May 1965 (Figure 8 and Tables 12 and 13) confirms the predominance of upbound coal shipments from the Ruhr (Orsoy, Lünen-Preussen, Bottrop, and Duisburg-Ruhrort), Dutch Limburg (Stein), and overseas (Rotterdam, Sluiskil, and Antwerp), and of downbound steel and slag shipments to overseas (Antwerp, Ghent, and Rotterdam) and West German (Mannheim, Karlstadt, Stuttgart, and Mainz) markets. Even after a decade of traffic on the canalized Moselle, it is too early to judge whether or not the relative importance of these ports will change, e.g., Antwerp vs. Rotterdam, but so far the pre-canalization pattern has not been altered.

SHORT-TERM PROSPECTS

It is difficult to forecast future developments on the Moselle on the basis of existing evidence. It is certain that traffic will increase after the current initial period of slow growth and adjustment to the new transport conditions.[12] But

12 J.-P. Seureau, "La Moselle canalisée et l'économie lorraine"; and M. Ruscher, "Situation et perspectives du trafic sur la Moselle canalisée," *RNIR* **40**, no. 8 (1968): 279-92.

perhaps the greatest unknown in the forecast is the future improvement of the Moselle south of Metz: begun in 1968, this project was completed by the end of 1973 as far as Pompey and Frouard at the junction with the Marne-Rhine Canal, and work was underway between Pompey and Neuves-Maisons; farther south, the Moselle-Saône deep-draft link is under study but no precise target date has been set so far for the completion of this section. The 1973 traffic data for the Moselle between Metz and Epinal (Table 6) indicate that such improvements are necessary if the waterway is expected to play more than a strictly regional role. It is likely that the European Investment Bank (a specialized agency of the EEC) will finance part of the cost of these improvements. Statistics dating back to 1850, although fragmentary and difficult to compare (on account of varying definitions and numerous boundary changes), show that for most of the Moselle River south of Metz, the greatest volumes of traffic were reached around 1900, when the Franco-German border bisecting Lorraine had shifted the focus of French economic activity from Metz to Nancy. Since then, the waterways of that area have stagnated, except for the Marne-Rhine Canal which has been improved somewhat and which still carries considerable volumes of traffic (Table 6). Only with a deep-draft Moselle-Saône link can the Moselle fulfill its basic threefold function — as a carrier of bulky materials and products (which it already is north of Metz), as a factor of interregional complementarity (between Lorraine and other regions to the north and south), and as a catalyst for regional development, be it in the Eifel-Hunsrück region of West Germany, or in the Vosges-Haute-Saône region of eastern France.

136

VII
Conclusion

While it might have been worthwhile to insist more upon the technical characteristics and economic consequences of the canalized Moselle River, this study has deliberately focussed on the historical-political-geographic aspects of the project. The scholar, unlike the journalist, has an obligation to be as objective as possible and to discuss all sides of a problem on the basis of existing evidence. When such evidence is too fragmentary or biased, it is preferable not to rely on it, and the latter course has been chosen in this study, despite the temptation to elaborate upon some post- World War II polemics.

Much was said and written, but little done, about the vital necessity to improve navigation on the Moselle River for nineteen centuries. Regional, national, and international rivalries were always at the root of the Moselle problem, even after the project had been completed. However, during those periods in which a strong central authority ruled the area now known as Lorraine, the river was improved, commerce on it flourished, and such cities as Metz and Trier became among Europe's leading trade centers. In more troubled periods of war and protectionism, the value of the river was essentially strategic and trade became almost non-existent, except for local traffic and military supplies. In the first case, one refers to the Roman and early medieval periods and to the period 1815-70; in the second case, one thinks of the seventeenth century with Louis XIV's wars, the French Revolution and Napoleonic period, as well as all subsequent periods of armed conflict. This characterization of the river's functions applies largely to the period before heavy industry, i.e., before 1870. Beginning with the 1850s, railroad construction and expansion of pig-iron and steel manufacturing resulted in a decline of the waterway's relative importance and the near-monopoly of rail transport, even though the waterway still managed to keep a sizable share of traffic in some commodities such as coal and steel products. Statistical evidence for the period 1850-1913 points to the fact that, in France at least, there was a deliberately balanced public works investment policy which tried to favor both waterways and railroads, although the latter retained their initial leading position in transporting the raw materials and products of heavy industry. Recent events have indicated that the railroads are still trying to retain their near-monopoly, but they are increasingly being challenged by road, water, and pipeline transport, more economical in many cases.

In the case of the Moselle, political factors have been far more important than economic conditions or the state of technology during given periods. First of all, territorial changes have obviously had an effect of varying nature on the river's traffic, but on the whole they meant war, conquest, boundary adjustments, and new customs barriers. The result was therefore generally negative. Secondly, even under strong central authority, local princes often took advantage of river traffic by exacting outrageous tolls as a convenient source of revenue. Even after the proclamation of the free navigation principle in 1792, it took two decades of French conquests to enforce it over most of Western Europe. Since 1815, the principle has been extended from the Rhine to most of the continent's large waterways, but policies vary in each case and tolls are still levied on some rivers, e.g., the Main, Moselle, and Neckar. Thirdly, in the centralized nation-states of the period 1870-1945, the predominant economic orientation changed from north-south to east-west. This change was largely due to the consolidation of the Rhine frontier in northeastern France from the reign of Louis XIV to the Napoleonic Empire, which reoriented French economic flows along a Le Havre-Paris-Nancy-Strasbourg axis. Likewise, the rise of Prussia as the dominant German state and its eastward push meant that, following the main economic axis of Germany, the Mittelland Canal linked the Ruhr with Berlin and the Oder, at the expense of the traditionally dominant Rhine valley. Only since 1945 has there been a serious attempt to revert to the north-south orientation, because Germany has lost its eastern provinces to Poland, and the division of Germany has cut off traffic on the upper Elbe and the eastern half of the Mittelland Canal. Moreover, until very recently, the Danube, also split by the Iron Curtain, has ceased to be a truly international waterway. Finally, the creation of the ECSC and EEC has intensified trade between France and Italy on the one hand and Benelux and West Germany on the other. At the same time, the Rhine has once again become the "main street of Europe" and there are numerous plans to link it southward to Marseilles.[1]

1 Aloys Michel, "The Canalization of the Moselle and West European Integration," *Geographical Review, 52*, no. 4 (1962), 490-1.

Therefore, as this study has tried to show, the Moselle has been more often than not a bone of contention between rival political units from the Roman period down to the present. Few were the periods when traffic on it was really important. The 1772 reports to the Société Royale des Sciences et Arts de Metz, as well as many other significant documents, have repeatedly shown that political rather than physical or technological obstacles were chiefly responsible for the surprisingly limited role which the waterway has played in the regional, national, and European economies. Could canalization change this situation in the future? When, and in what respect?

The point of departure of this study was the statement that, in general, a navigable waterway should serve three purposes: transport of bulky goods, inter-regional complementarity, and regional development. Historical evidence in the case of the Moselle has shown that seldom were these aims achieved. But circumstances have changed radically since 1950, when the first step was taken towards uniting Europe without resorting to armed force. The climate of cooperation which has existed since should help the peoples of Europe to settle their differences and work for the common good of all, although national self-interest is still very much in evidence. In such a climate, a unified transport policy could be achieved, and within this policy transport structures (including the canalized Moselle) would have a leading role to play within the framework of economic and political integration.

The traffic function of the Moselle could be greatly expanded through diversification, but this can only came about once the deep-draft Moselle-Saône link is completed. It will then be possible to ship goods between Marseilles, Lyons, Metz, Cologne, and Rotterdam. This will mean increased trade between northern and southern Europe along the Saône-Rhône corridor, which is topographically the most convenient route between the Mediterranean and the North Sea. Of course, the Moselle is only one of three alternate routes between the Saône and the North Sea, and it will be essential in the near future to improve the Meuse and the Rhône-Rhine link (via the Doubs River), in order to give as many regions as possible a chance to benefit from an increase in north-south trade. Critics of such a large-scale waterways plan point out that competition from other means of transport could well reduce the economic viability of the new river axis. They give the example of the Marseilles-Strasbourg-Karlsruhe crude petroleum pipeline, which would eventually monopolize all trade in this product along this axis. However, assuming that petroleum will remain an important energy source for some time, it is reasonable to believe that pipelines, no matter how large, are unlikely to satisfy all of Europe's oil needs. It is rather unfortunate that the emphasis is always placed upon competition rather than coordination of various means of transport, when the latter is not only desirable but necessary in many instances.

The other two functions of the canalized Moselle should logically follow from the first one. Interregional complementarity between the Ruhr and Lorraine or between the Benelux ports and Lorraine were discussed in connection with attitudes towards the final project from early times to the present. The often-mentioned notion of désenclavement is related to the idea of interregional complementarity. The new waterway extended southward should help increase complementarity precisely by breaking the isolation of some areas. Thus, désenclavement also implies opening hitherto isolated areas to industrial and commercial development. Some critics argue that the new waterway, far from developing less-favored regions along its course, has increased the advantage of the already well-developed regions. Certainly, the case of the Eifel-Hunsrück region seems to validate this argument, but it is still too early to assess the impact of the canalized Moselle in this particular instance. One needs only to observe the industrial boom in and around Trier since 1964 to realize that where local authorities are eager to promote development, the building of a new waterway cannot fail but to have a positive influence. On the other hand, one should not be overly optimistic in the short run because the derived effects of any new transport route will not be felt until many years have passed.

Even though predictions and forecasts should be made with the utmost caution, it is very likely that the Moselle will have an important role to play in an economically and politically united Europe. In fact, it can play such a role only if such a large framework exists, including standardized transport networks (witness the already discussed ECMT waterways network) and common transport policies with respect to legislation and conditions of competition. No problem can ever be solved separately from other problems; likewise, the importance of the Moselle is (and always has been) a function of the degree of cooperation and liberalism that the parties concerned will be (and have been) willing to accept.

The value of a study such as this is based on the hope that people as well as nations can learn from the lessons of history. There are many approaches to the problems of transportation geography. The historical approach has the advantage of hindsight: past experience can serve as a guideline or a warning for or against future action, and past events, attitudes, interrelations, and problems cannot be invalidated as readily as present or potential ones. It must be weighed against the contemporary trend of research concentration on mathematical models. There should be a place for both historical and quantitative approaches to the study of transportation geography and also for the more recent behavioral or systems approaches, all of which provide a greater understanding of the subject.

Statistical Appendix

TABLE 1   List of "Waterways of interest to Europe as a whole" drawn up by the ECMT in 1953 and amended in 1964

1   Improvement of the Dunkirk-Scheldt link and international extensions
2   Improvement of the Scheldt-Rhine link
3   Improvement of the Meuse and its international connections
4   Meuse-Rhine link, with connection to Aachen
5   *Canalization of the Moselle*
6   Improvement of navigation conditions on the Rhine between Strasbourg and St Goar
7   Rhône-Rhine link
8   Improvement of the Rhine between Basle and Lake Constance
9   Rhine-Main-Danube link
10   Improvement of the Elbe, with link from Hamburg to the inland waterways network of western Europe
11   Oder-Danube link
12   Link between Lake Maggiore and the Adriatic

SOURCE: CEMT, *Acte Final, Protocole, Règlement Intérieur, Résolutions: 1953* (Paris: 1954), p. 39; and CEMT, *Conseil des Ministres: Résolutions* XIV (1964), pp. 38-40 (Paris: 1965).

TABLE 2   ECMT list of dimensions for "European-draft" waterways and locks

	Waterways			Locks	
a width	28 m		a width	12 m	
b depth	3.5 m		b depth	3.5 m	
c minimum curve radius	800 m		c length	85 m	

SOURCE: CEMT, *Conseil des Ministres: Résolutions* II (1954), pp. 20-1
(Paris: 1955).

TABLE 3   ECMT classification of European inland waterways and
corresponding standard dimensions of craft

Class of waterway:

 I   300-ton draft
 II   600-ton draft
III 1000-ton draft
IV 1350-ton ("European") draft
 V   2000-ton draft
VI 3000-ton draft and deeper (dimensions not available)

Dimensions (Meters):

 a Length
 b Width
 c Draft
 d Headroom

	I	II	III	IV	V
a	38.5	50.0	67.0	80.0	95.0
b	5.0	6.6	8.2	9.5	11.0
c	2.2	2.5	2.5	2.5	2.7
d	3.55	4.2	3.95	4.4	6.7

SOURCE: CEMT, *Conseil des Ministres: Résolutions* XI (1961), p. 42
(Paris: 1962).

142

TABLE 4   Traffic flows of ECSC Treaty products within, to, and from north-eastern France, 1956 and 1964 (thousands of metric tons)

Legend:

A   Coal
B   Lignite
C   Coke
D   Iron ore
E   Managanese ore

F   Scrap
G   Pig-iron and crude steel
H   Semi-finished products
I   Rolled-steel products

X   Traffic within northeastern France
Y   Traffic from northeastern France towards other regions
Z   Traffic from other regions to northeastern France

	X	Y	Z
1956			
A	4,618	4,011	5,953
B	2	1	232
C	1,411	105	6,415
D	12,111	17,100	162
E	9	17	148
F	523	165	1,014
G	609	489	303
H	810	828	297
I	968	4,649	369
TOTAL:	21,061	27,365	14,893
1964			
A	6,358	3,986	6,276
B	5	1	345
C	2,471	217	6,076
D	16,298	15,640	665
E	3	5	140
F	585	260	790
G	645	298	383
H	786	1,237	785
I	1,335	5,876	872
TOTAL:	28,486	27,520	16,332

SOURCES: *For 1956:* "Résultats de la statistique des transports des produits du traité: année 1956," *Informations Statistiques* V, no. 1 (January-February 1958): Tables 13-21, pp. 80-97 (published by CECA, Haute Autorité, Luxembourg). *For 1964:* OSCE, *Transports des produits du Traité de la CECA: année 1964* (Brussels-Luxembourg: 1966), separate tables nos. Ib-Xb, pp. 86-95.

TABLE 5   Evolution of rail transport costs for coke from the Ruhr to
Lorraine, 1953-1964

A   Dates of railroad rate changes since the establishment of the common market for coal on 10 February 1953
B   Selling price of coke, including transport costs (in Deutsche Mark per
metric ton; 1 DM equals about US$4)
C   Cost of transporting one metric ton of coke in complete 1000-ton trains
from Gelsenkirchen (Ruhr) to Homécourt (Lorraine), in DM
D   Share of transport costs over selling price (C/B), in per cent

A	B	C	D
10 Feb. 1953:	65.00	26.54	41
1 Nov. 1954:	61.17	24.09	39
1 May 1955:	61.10	20.63	34
1 May 1956:	68.19	20.53	30
1 Oct. 1957:	80.44	19.58	24
1 Sept. 1960:	80.11	20.85	26
1 Nov. 1960:	80.11	18.45	23
1 Mar. 1962:	80.11	16.33	20.3
1 Oct. 1962:	82.18	16.20	19.8
1 Jul. 1963:	83.71	17.06	20.4
1 Sept. 1964:	85.60	15.92	18.6

SOURCE: Data appended to a letter from Mr I. Debois, Director, *Direction de
des Transports, Direction Générale Economie et Energie, Haute Autorité,*
CECA, Luxembourg, 20 Oct. 1965.

LEGEND FOR TABLES 6 and 7
French Moselle: sections of the waterway, from north to south

A   Canalized Moselle from the Franco-German border at Apach to Thionville; in use since
June 1964.

B   Canalized Moselle from Thionville to Metz (formerly known as CAMIFEMO or Canal
des Mines de Fer de la Moselle) (Moselle Iron Mines Canal); in use since 1932,
improved in 1964.

C   Canalized Moselle from Metz to Frouard; in use since 1842, improved between 1867
and 1878, and between 1964 and 1969.

D   Marne-Rhine Canal from Laneuveville to Toul (parallel to the Meurthe and Moselle
rivers); in use since 1853, improved during the 1960s.

E   Canal de l'Est (southern branch), from Toul to Messein (parallel to the Moselle
river); in use since 1882, improved between 1969 and 1973.

F   Canal de l'Est (southern branch), from Messein to the Saône River (parallel in part to
the Moselle River); in use since 1882, being improved between 1972 and 1980.

144

G Canal de l'Est (Nancy branch), from the Marne-Rhine Canal at Laneuveville to the
Canal de l'Est (southern branch) at Messein; in use since 1882, no information available
as to future improvement.

TABLE 6 Traffic on the French Moselle for selected years, 1850-1973

	Metric tons	Ton-kilometers
1850: C[a]	47,078	5,508,240
D[c]	1,770	21,320
1870: C[a]	12,676	174,619
D[c,d,e]	391,165	3,358,253
1885: C[b]	169,273	2,021,582
D[f]	1,596,470	127,537,726
E[h]	408,609	18,508,543
F[h]	408,609	18,508,543
G	212,908	2,049,781
1913: C[b]	554,604	7,473,958
D[f]	4,475,141	327,989,677
E	1,209,996	20,006,613
F	803,152	68,950,386
G	774,481	7,707,304
1930: C	802,298	10,647,662
D[g]	4,528,915	292,558,710
E	727,569	9,269,577
F	570,093	46,616,703
G	819,747	8,162,005
1938: B	983,923	20,798,132
C	1,527,720	54,155,542
D[e]	5,028,391	512,760,102
E	707,237	13,236,738
F	737,183	72,539,825
G	615,826	6,121,946
1950: B	634,357	10,465,745
C	978,375	28,717,359
D	2,409,773	66,180,771
E	390,838	5,926,923
F	483,771	23,578,803
G	463,594	4,635,940
1957: B	1,113,577	23,584,259
C	1,799,170	54,828,817
D	3,472,641	92,247,351
E	726,639	8,935,414
F	558,286	40,158,199
G	659,273	6,592,730

TABLE 6   continued

		Metric tons	Ton-kilometers
1964:	A	844,712	22,807,224
	B	1,747,887	24,523,774
	C	1,374,650	46,561,783
	D	3,582,710	99,039,123
	E	698,115	13,300,298
	F	621,558	57,426,437
	G	399,476	3,994,760
1965:	A	3,209,389	86,653,503
	B	4,006,593	37,272,030
	C	1,191,789	41,040,419
	D	3,384,054	99,004,816
	E	567,148	11,779,894
	F	473,706	43,963,028
	G	318,995	3,115,070
1973:	A		
	B	8,068,370	292,686,097
	C	1,406,185	54,361,866
	D — Laneuveville-Frouard	1,463,219	20,009,571
	— Frouard-Toul	1,532,982	35,221,013
	E	576,309	8,943,855
	F	555,498	61,256,070
	G	399,869	3,996,359

SOURCE: France, Ministère des Transports et Ministère de l'Equipement, ONN, *Statistique annuelle de la navigation intérieure* (Paris: annual publication), for 1973 data; *idem, Statistique annuelle de la navigation intérieure par sections de voies navigables* (Paris: annual publication), for 1964 and 1965 data; data from 1850 to 1957: courtesy of the Director of the ONN.

NOTES:

a From Apach (present Franco-German border) to Frouard
b From Arnaville (1871-1918 border) to Frouard
c Meurthe River from Laneuveville to Frouard
d 1870 data for the Meurthe from Laneuveville to Frouard; 3950 metric tons and 36,172 ton-kilometers
e For the whole Marne-Rhine Canal (from Vitry to Strasbourg)
f From Vitry to the 1871-1918 Franco-German border
g From Vitry to Dombasle; 1930 data for Dombasle-Strasbourg section of the canal: 2,453,090 metric tons and 177,139,758 ton-kilometers
h From Toul to the Saône River, i.e., sections (E) and (F)

146

TABLE 7   Traffic of the major French Moselle ports, 1973
(in metric tons; ports ranked from north to south, by section)

A	Koenigsmacker	170,061
	Thionville-Illange	3,544,099
B	Mondelange-Richemont	2,150,649
	Hagondange	668,323
C	Metz	695,665
	Pagny-sur-Moselle	150,842
	Pont-à-Mousson	100,408
	Dieulouard	275,157
D	(none)	
E	Maron	262,200
	Neuves-Maisons	158,100

SOURCE: France, Ministère des Transports et Ministère de l'Equipement, ONN, *Statistique annuelle de la navigation intérieure 1973* (Paris: 1974), Part 5, Table B, pp. 344-89.

TABLE 8   Official 1955 traffic estimates for the canalized Moselle's first full year of operation

		'000 metric tons
1	**Upbound traffic:**	
	Coal, coke, and lignite	4,050
	High-grade iron ore	300
	Manganese ore	150
	Scrap	100
	Other products	100
		4,700
2	**Downbound traffic:**	
	Iron and steel products	1,850
	Coal from the Saar and Lorraine	700
	Lumber and lumber products	450
	Slag from the blast-furnaces	450
	Wheat	300
	Cement	250
	Other products	250
		4,250
3	**Local traffice between Trier and Koblenz**	**1,000**
	TOTAL:	**9,950**

SOURCE: France, Ministère des Affaires Etrangères, *Rapport de la Commission franco-allemande pour l'étude de la canalisation de la Moselle* (Paris: Imprimerie Nationale, 1956), pp. 186-96. These were the French delegation's estimates, the Germans' figures being much lower.

TABLE 9   Annual traffic on the canalized Moselle River, 1964-1973: total traffic at the Franco-German border, to and from French ports (in metric tons)

	Total traffic	Annual increase (+ or -) (%)
1964[1]	834,982	—
1965	3,210,808	—[2]
1966	4,014,886	+ 25.04
1967	4,671,548	+ 16.36
1968	5,821,645	+ 24.62
1969	6,535,162	+ 12.26
1970	7,792,072	+ 19.23
1971	7,501,713	− 3.73
1972	6,986,660	− 6.87
1973	7,630,538	+ 9.22

Notes: 1   June through December
2   1965/64 increase cannot be calculated because of different time periods

SOURCE: *Revue de la Navigation Fluviale Européenne,* vols **37-46** (1965-74).

TABLE 10   Total traffic to and from French ports at the Franco-German border, 1965 and 1973

	Upbound		Downbound	
	1965	1973	1965	1973
Total traffic: (metric tons)	1,609,980	3,991,193	1,600,828	3,639,345
Goods carried: (per cent)				
Mineral fuels	87.6	66.6	—	—
Iron and manganese ores	—	19.1	—	—
Scrap	2.4	1.0	—	0.2
Iron and steel products	3.0	5.7	68.6	30.0
Sand, gravel, and slag	—	0.4	27.6	38.5
Grains	—	—	—	22.5
Other products	7.0	7.2	3.8	8.8
	100.0	100.0	100.0	100.0

SOURCE: *RNIR*, **38**, 3 (1966): 82, and *Revue de la Navigation Fluviale Européenne,* **46**, 5 (1974): 148-9.

TABLE 11   Total traffic at the Koblenz locks, 1965 and 1973

	Upbound		Downbound	
	1965	1973	1965	1973
Total traffic:				
(metric tons)	2,669,100	6,312,000	1,929,700	4,250,000
Goods carried:				
Mineral fuels	58.9	47.6	0.1	0.4
Liquid fuels	22.8	19.4	1.4	1.2
Sand, gravel, and slag	10.2	6.0	35.6	38.1
Ores and scrap	3.1	15.4	0.5	0.3
Iron and steel products	1.8	3.3	59.0	32.5
Other products	3.2	8.3	3.4	27.5
	100.0	100.0	100.0	100.0
Origin or destination:	'000 metric tons		Per cent	
(both directions)				
France	3,265	7,123	70.9	67.5
Luxembourg	117	1,406	2.6	13.3
Koblenz area ports	847	985	18.5	9.3
Other German ports	370	1,049	8.0	9.9
Nationalities of craft				
(both directions) Per cent				
West German	40.7			44.9
French	32.1			23.4
Dutch	12.4			16.0
Belgian	11.7			11.3
Swiss	2.1			3.3
Luxembourg	0.8			1.0
Other	0.2			0.1

SOURCE: *RNIR*, **38**, 4 (1966): 107, and *Revue de la Navigation Fluviale Européenne,* **46**, 5 (1974): 148-9.

150

TABLE 12   Total traffic at the Franco-German border by major port of origin outside France, June 1964 to May 1965 (in metric tons; ports shipping over 10,000 tons)

B   Belgian port
NL Dutch ports
D   West German ports

			Main product shipped
D	Orsoy	297,773	Solid fuels
D	Lünen-Preussen	174,571	Solid fuels
NL	Rotterdam	138,250	Solid fuels
NL	Stein	82,206	Solid fuels
NL	Sluiskil	78,759	Solid fuels
D	Duisburg-Ruhrort	48,745	Steel plate
D	Bottrop	46,766	Solid fuels
B	Antwerp	20,756	Sulphur
D	Beddingen-Salzgitter	16,968	Steel products
D	Homberg	14,774	Solid fuels
D	Stumm	10,616	Solid fuels
D	Hamm	10,554	Solid fuels

All other ports of origin outside France + Strasbourg (56 ports):	102,435
of which (D) (29 ports):	53,587
(NL) (19 ports):	22,104
(B) (7 ports):	22,183
(France) (1 port):	4,561
TOTAL:	1,043,173

SOURCE: *RNIR*, vols **36**, no. 13 (1964) to **37**, no. 11 (1965), tables entitled "Ports de la Moselle," published fortnightly in the section entitled "Le trafic dans le bassin du Rhin et en Belgique."

TABLE 13   Total traffic at the Franco-German border by major port of destination outside France, June 1964 to May 1965 (in metric tons; ports receiving over 10,000 tons)

B Belgian ports
NL Dutch ports
D West German ports
CH Swiss port

			Main product(s) shipped
B	Antwerp	344,742	Steel products
B	Ghent	84,465	Steel products
D	Mannheim	76,988	Slag and steel products
D	Karlstadt	55,117	Slag
D	Amöneburg	54,333	Slag
D	Duisburg-Ruhrort	46,312	Steel products
NL	Rotterdam	40,111	Steel products
CH	Basle	34,297	Steel products
D	Stuttgart	26,065	Slag
D	Mainz	25,052	Slag
D	Cologne	18,894	Steel products
D	Dortmund	18,544	Steel products
D	Hamm	17,457	Steel products
D	Eberbach	16,649	Steel products
D	Wiesbaden	13,578	Slag
D	Frankfurt am Main	13,562	Steel products
D	Beddingen-Salzgitter	12,199	Steel products
D	Andernach	11,182	Slag and barley
D	Heilbronn	10,088	Steel products

All other ports of destination outside	
France + Strasbourg (104 ports):	161,969
of which (D) (59 ports):	107,482
(NL) (38 ports):	46,371
(B) (6 ports):	8,112
(France) (1 port):	4
TOTAL:	1,081,604

SOURCE: See Table 12.

TABLE 14   Total traffic at the Franco-German border by major upbound commodity,
June 1964 to May 1965 (in metric tons; shipments of over 2000 tons per commodity)

		Leading port of origin	
Solid fuels	866,183	D	Orsoy
Scrap	46,717	NL	Rotterdam
Steel plate	37,408	D	Duisburg-Ruhrort
Steel products	26,650	D	Schwelgern
Sulphur	19,090	B	Antwerp
Steel coils	7,957	D	Beddingen-Salzgitter
Ferro-phosphorus	6,191	NL	Rotterdam
Iron ore	4,192	D	Emden
Manganese ore	3,652	NL	Rotterdam
Magnesia	3,604	NL	Rotterdam
Diesel fuel	3,317	F	Strasbourg
Chromium ore	2,696	NL	Rotterdam
All other products:	15,516 (30 groups)		
TOTAL:	1,043,173		

SOURCE: See Table 12.

TABLE 15   Total traffic at the Franco-German border by major downbound commodity,
June 1964 to May 1965 (in metric tons; shipments of over 2000 tons per commodity)

		Leading port of destination	
Steel products	781,494	B	Antwerp
Blast-furnace slag	246,543	D	Karlstadt
Sulphuric acid	8,366	D	Leverkusen
Ferro-manganese	5,250	D	Duisburg-Ruhrort
Barley	4,631	D	Andernach
Steel wire	4,399	D	Dortmund
Firewood billets	4,320	D	Cologne
Ferro-silicium	4,281	D	Duisburg-Ruhrort
Rough timber	2,805	D	Ludwigshafen
Sodium carbonate	2,588	NL	Rotterdam
All other products	16,927 (22 groups)		
TOTAL	1,081,604		

SOURCE: See Table 12.

153

TABLE 16 Total cost of the Moselle canalization project (in millions of Deutsche Mark)

A In West Germany
B In France
C In the German-Luxembourg border section
D Total

	A	B	C	D
Projects and groundwork	4.3	0.7	0.1	5.1
Purchase of land and indemnizations	30.5	1.7	0.9	33.1
Locks and dams	236.0	31.2	(a)	267.2
Dredging operations and removal of rocks from riverbed	248.0	42.0	2.2	292.2
Buildings	2.1	0.6	0.7	3.4
Riverbank protection	89.0	4.9	8.5	102.4
Ancillary work	(b)	(b)	(b)	11.6
Operating expenses	(b)	(b)	(b)	65.0
TOTAL	(b)	(b)	(b)	780.0

(a) Included in A
(b) Not available
In the 1960s, 1 Deutsche Mark equalled about US $4.00.

SOURCE: Charles Chevrier and Hans Bormann, "Les travaux d'aménagement de la Moselle" (French/German), *Der Ausbau der Mosel / L'aménagement de la Moselle* (Trier: SIM, 1966), p. 76.

Selected Bibliography

"Une artère fluviale de développement: la Moselle; situation et perspectives."
RNIR **40**, no. 8 (1968): 246-92. Special issue.

Bégin, E.-A. *Metz depuis 18 siècles*. 3 vols. Metz, 1845.

Béthémont, Jacques. "Un problème français à l'échelle européenne: la liaison
Méditerranée-Mer du Nord." *Revue de Géographie de Lyon* **38**, no. 4 (1963):
315-56.

Bonét-Maury, C. (editor). *Les Actes du Rhin et de la Moselle: Traités, Conventions, Lois et Règlements principaux concernant la navigation sur le Rhin et les voies navigables d'Europe occidentale*. 3rd ed. revised (1st ed.: 1947; 2nd ed.: 1957). Strasbourg: Les Editions de la Navigation du Rhin, 1966.

Cermakian, Jean. "Europe's Inland Waterways." *California Engineer* **44**, no. 3
(1965): 12-15 and 30-31.

–. "The European Inland Waterways Network: A Case-Study in the Geography
of European Cooperation." *Yearbook of the Association of Pacific Coast
Geographers* **28** (1966): 175-80.

–. "La Moselle canalisée et la voie maritime du Saint-Laurent: notes comparatives." *Cahiers de Géographie de Québec* **11**, no. 23 (September 1967):
253-75. English summary, p. 274.

Chambre de Commerce de Metz. *La Chambre de Commerce de Metz:
1815-1922*. Metz, 1922.

Chanrion, Fernand. *Une victoire européenne: la Moselle*. Paris: Berger-Levrault,
1964.

CECA. Haute Autorité *CECA 1952-1962: résultats, limites, perspectives*. Luxembourg, 1963.

CEE. Commission. *Mémorandum sur l'orientation à donner à la politique commune des transports.* Brussels, 1961. (Mimeographed.)

⁻. *Rapport sur la situation de l'infrastructure et du parc des transports dans la Communauté.* Vol. 3: *Navigation intérieure.* Brussels, 1962. (Mimeographed.)

⁻. *Recommandations de la Commission en vue du développement de l'infrastructure des transports dans le cadre de la Communauté.* Brussels, 1960-61. (Mimeographed.)

CEMT. *Acte final, protocole, règlement intérieur, résolutions: Bruxelles, le 17 octobre 1953.* Paris, 1954. In French and English.

⁻. *Conseil des Ministres: Résolutions.* Vols 2-23 (1954-73). In French or English. Paris, 1955-74.

⁻. *Rapport annuel.* Vols 1-20 (1954-73). In French or English. Paris, 1955-74.

"Convention du 27 octobre 1956 entre la République Française, la République Fédérale d'Allemagne, et le Grand-Duché de Luxembourg au sujet de la canalisation de la Moselle." *Journal Officiel* (France), 10 January 1957; *Bundesgesetzblatt* (West Germany), 24 December 1956; *Mémorial* (Luxembourg), 29 December 1956. In French or German.

Degott, Jean. *La canalisation de la Moselle dans l'économie du charbon et de l'acier.* Metz, 1961. (Mimeographed doctoral dissertation, Université de Strasbourg, Faculté de Droit et des Sciences Politiques.)

Delmer, A. "Les voies navigables reliant la Mer du Nord à la Méditerranée: voies alsacienne, lorraine, ardennaise." *Bulletin de la Société Belge d'Etudes Géographiques* **31**, no. 1 (1962): 73-86.

France. Ministère des Affaires Etrangères. *Rapport de la Commission franco-allemande pour l'étude de la canalisation de la Moselle.* Paris: Imprimerie Nationale, 1956.

France. Ministère de l'Equipement. ONN. *Statistique annuelle de la navigation intérieure par courants de trafic;* and *Statistique annuelle de la navigation intérieure par sections de voies navigables.* Paris: ONN; annual publications, replaced in 1971 by a single annual volume entitled *Statistique annuelle de la navigation intérieure.*

France. Rapport du Group de Travail au Premier Ministre. "L'axe de transport par voie d'eau entre le Nord-Est de la France et la Méditerranée." *Notes et Etudes Documentaires,* no. 2,874 (2 April 1962). Periodical issued by La Documentation Française, the governmental information agency, in Paris.

Gerges, Martin (editor). *La Moselle: son passé, son avenir.* Schwebsingen, Luxembourg: Imprimerie Bourg-Bourger, 1958. Texts in French or German.

Houpert, Albert. *La Moselle navigable: des Nautae gallo-romains au CAMIFEMO.* Metz: Chambre de Commerce de Metz, 1932.

Kish, George. "Transportation within the European Economic Community: Problems and Policies." *The East Lakes Geographer* no. 1 (November 1964).

Labasse, Jean, *L'organisation de l'espace: éléments de géographie volontaire.* Paris: Hermann, 1966.

Labaste, André. "Les relations par voie ferrée entre l'Est et le Nord de la France." *Annales de Géographie* **41**, no. 232 (1932): 233-41.

Lister, Louis. *Europe's Coal and Steel Community.* New York: Praeger, 1960.

Michel, Aloys A. "The Canalization of the Moselle and West European Integration." *Geographical Review* **52**, no. 4 (1962): 475-91.

Michelet, Pierre. *Les transports au sol et l'organisation de l'Europe.* Paris: Payot, 1962.

"La Moselle: nouvelle voie navigable européenne." *RNIR* **36**, no. 10 (1964): 370-420. Special issue.

OSCE. "Statistique annuelle." *Transports.* Brussels and Luxembourg, annual since 1964, beginning with statistics for the year 1962. In German, French, Italian, and Dutch.

–. *Transports des produits du Traité de la CECA.* Brussels and Luxembourg, annual since 1957, beginning with statistics for the year 1956. In French, German, Italian, or Dutch.

Pounds, Norman J.G. "Lorraine and the Ruhr." *Economic Geography* **33**, no. 2 (1957): 149-62.

Pounds, Norman J.G., and Parker, William N. *Coal and Steel in Western Europe.* Bloomington: Indiana University Press, 1957.

Prêcheur, Claude. *La Lorraine sidérurgique.* 2 vols. Paris: SABRI, 1959.

–. "La via navigabile Lorena-Mediterraneo." *Bollettino della Società Geografica Italiana,* Series 9, **3**, nos. 4-6 (April-June 1962): 137-67. English summary, p. 167.

Renouard, Dominique. *Les transports de marchandises par fer, route et eau depuis 1850.* Paris: Fondation Nationale des Sciences Politiques, *Revue de la Navigation Intérieure et Rhinane.* Strasbourg: Les Editions de la Navigation du Rhin, since 1922 (bimonthly). From 1969, becomes *Revue de la Navigation Fluviale Européenne.*

Scharff, Viktor. *Die Moselkanal: eine wirtschaftliche und politische Notwendigkeit.* Trier, 1904 (privately published).

Schumacher, Hermann. *Die westdeutsche Eisenindustrie und die Moselkanalisierung.* Leipsig, 1910.

Société du Port Fluvial de Mertert S.A. *Le port de Mertert et la navigation de la Moselle.* Luxembourg: Imprimerie Bourg-Bourger, 1966.

Société Internationale de la Moselle (G.m.b.H.) / Internationale Mosel-Gesellschaft m.b.H. *Der Ausbau der Mosel / L'aménagement de la Moselle.* ("Plaquette éditée par la Société Internationale de la Moselle à l'occasion de l'inauguration de la Moselle canalisée.") Trier: SIM, 1964. In German and French.

−. *Der Ausbau der Mosel zwischen Diedenhofen und Koblenz / L'aménagement de la Moselle entre Thionville et Coblence.* Trier: SIM, 1966. In German and French.

−. *Geschäftsbericht / Rapport de Gestion.* Annual since 1958 (for the year 1957). Trier: SIM. In German and French.

Thomas, Abel. *Sillon rhodanien − Axe Rhin-Méditerranée.* Paris: Ministère de la Construction, 1960. Aménagement du Territoire. Rapport du Commissaire à l'Aménagement du Territoire.

United Nations. Economic Commission for Europe. *Annual Bulletin of Transport Statistics for Europe / Bulletin annuel de statistiques de transports européens.* Vols 1-23 (1949-71). Geneva or New York: UN, 1950-73. In English and French (also Russian from 1968).

Vadot, Robert. "La modernisation du Canal de l'Est (Branche Sud)." *RNIR* **30**, no. 6 (1958): 206-13.

Valle, Carlo della. "Il Canale dalla Marna al Reno e la navigazione interna nella Lorena." *Bollettino della Società Geografica Italiana*, Series 8, **11**, nos. 1-3 (January-March 1958): 53-73. English summary, p. 73.

Voies Navigables du Bassin Lorrain, Commission des. *La voie navigable Lorraine-Méditerranée.* Nancy: Commission des Voies Navigables du Bassin Lorrain, Nancy; 1959.

Wasser- und Schiffahrtsdirektion Mainz. Neubauabteilung für den Ausbau der Mosel, Trier, and Service de la Navigation de Nancy, Arrondissement spécial de Thionville. *Die Mosel von Thionville bis Koblenz: Schiffahrtskarte / La Moselle de Thionville à Koblenz: carte de la navigation.* Trier: SIM, 1964. Boatmen's atlas. Scale of base maps: 1:10,000. Legends and captions in German and French.

Zentral-Kommission für die Rheinschiffahrt. *Rheinurkunden.* 2 vols. The Hague, Munich, and Leipzig: Central Rhine Commission, 1918. Introduction in German and Dutch, notes in German, and original texts in French, German, or Dutch.

Résumé

L'auteur de cet ouvrage part du principe qu'une voie navigable à grand gabarit devrait posséder trois fonctions principales: transport de produits pondéreux, renforcement de la complémentarité entre deux ou plusieurs régions, et contribution à un meilleur aménagement de l'espace géo-économique. Cette troisième fonction est explicitée par un terme utilisé par bon nombre de géographes francophones, celui de *désenclavement,* à savoir l'opération qui consiste à mettre fin à l'isolement socio-économique d'une région à l'intérieur d'un contexte national ou international de prospérité et de croissance économiques.

L'analyse des données statistiques et des rapports concernant les transports en Europe, au cours de la période 1950-74, confirme cette triple vocation de la voie navigable à grand gabarit. Cependant, on ne peut en dire de même de la navigation intérieure européenne avant cette période. A cause de la complexité des événements historiques servant de toile de fond à cette étude, et en raison du fait que ce sont des obstacles de nature politique et militaire, beaucoup plus que des barrières économiques ou technologiques, qui ont freiné dans bien des cas le développement de la triple vocation des voies navigables, cet ouvrage a été bâti selon un modèle historique-politique-géographique. Cela ne signifie point que les facteurs d'ordre économique et technologique n'ont pas été pris en considération. Mais ces facteurs sont utilisés ici uniquement à titre d'éléments dans une analyse complexe. Cette approche méthodologique peut sembler subjective, mais l'auteur n'avait pas d'autre choix, étant donné la nature de la documentation existante. De plus, l'auteur ne prétend pas que cette étude présente la seule méthodologie possible en géographie des transports, car l'approche dépend nécessairement du problème à l'étude.

Pour toutes les raisons mentionnées ci-dessus, l'ouvrage suit un plan chronologique plutôt que thématique. Dans cette perspective, il y a deux dates qui sont des années-pivots dans l'histoire de l'évolution de l'idée de libre navigation en Europe: en 1815, le principe de la libre navigation fut accepté et institutionnalisé pour la première fois par les principaux Etats européens au Congrès de Vienne; en 1945, au terme de la deuxième guerre mondiale, dans un contexte totalement nouveau de coopération bâtie sur les ruines de l'Europe occidentale à la suite de la division entre l'Est et l'Ouest, les débuts du mouvement favorable à l'intégration économique et politique de l'Europe rendirent possible l'élaboration d'une politique commune des transports, politique qui comprend la construction de réseaux d'intérêt européen.

L'auteur, en tant que géographe, se devait également d'étudier l'influence de l'utilisation (ou de la non-utilisation) de la Moselle sur la population et l'économie des régions qu'elle traverse. Aussi a-t-il insisté sur cet aspect du problème dans le cadre de chacune des périodes étudiées, en terminant par un bilan de la première décénnie de la Moselle canalisée et une tentative de projection vers l'avenir. C'est ainsi que l'auteur analyse une seconde dimension géographique, à savoir la fonction vitale de la Moselle comme l'un des trois grands axes fluviaux entre la Méditerranée et la Mer du Nord (les deux autres étant la Meuse et le canal du Rhône au Rhin), avec toutes les conséquences qu'une telle fonction a pu (et pourrait) avoir sur le trafic et les autres fonctions de ce cours d'eau.

En dernier lieu, cette étude vise à démontrer que cette voie navigable à vocation internationale a été sous-utilisée jusqu'à ces dernières années en raison de querelles et de rivalités politiques parfois vieilles de plusieurs siècles.

Zusammenfassung

Der Ausgangspunkt diser Monographie ist die Forderung, eine Gross-Schiffahrtsstrasse habe drei Funktionen zu erfüllen: den Transport von Massengütern, die
Intensivierung räumlicher Ergänzung und einen Beitrag zu einer rationelleren
regionalen Entwicklung. Die Rolle der letzteren Funktion wird deutlicher, wenn
man das von französisch-sprechenden Geographen formulierte Konzept des "désenclavement" heranziecht, d.h. die Auflösung der räumlichen und sozialen Isolation in Verbindung mit nationalem oder internationalem Wirtschaftswachstum.

Diese drei Funktionen der Gross-Schiffahrtsstrasse lassen sich durch die Analyse
der europäischen Verkehrsstatistik und Berichte für die Periode 1950-1974 klar
zeigen. Das gleiche lässt sich aber von der europäischen Binnenschiffahrt vor dieser
Periode nicht sagen. Wegen des komplizierten geschichtlichen Hintergrunds, auf
dem sich diese Untersuchung hervorhebt, und weil politische und militärische
Hindernisse, eher als wirtschaftliche und technologische, der Entwicklung der
dreifachen Funktion der Wasserstrasse öfters im Wege standen, wurde ein
geschichtlich-politisch-geographischer Forschungsansatz gewählt. Das bedeudet
nicht, dass wirtschaftliche und technologische Faktoren nicht in Betracht gezogen
wurden, sondern dass sie nur als Bausteine in einer ziemlich komplizierten Analyse
gebraucht wurden. Dieser Forschungsansatz dürfte wohl etwas einseitig er-
scheinen: er war aber auch unvermeidlich wegen der Natur der vorliegenden Daten.
Der Verfasser behauptet nicht, dass diese Untersuchung die einzige Verfahrens-
weise in der Verkehrsgeographie anbietet; die Methode hängt motwendigerweise
von dem Wesen des jeweils in Betracht stehenden Problems ab.

Aus allen oben erwähnten Gründen folgt die Untersuchung einem chrono-
logischen, nicht einem thematischen, Umriss. Wenn man das Problem in diesem

Licht sieht, darf man zwei Daten als Wendepunkte in der Evolutionsgeschichte der Idee der freien Navigation in Europa betrachten: im Jahre 1815 wurde das Prinzip der Freien Navigation zum ersten Mal von allen wichtigen europäischen Staaten auf dem Wiener Kongress bestätigt und kodifiziert; im Jahr 1945, am Ende des zweiten Weltkrieges und in dem völlig neuen Klima der Zusammenarbeit, das sich aus den Ruinen Westeuropas und den Folgen der Ost-West-Spaltung entwickelte, machten die Anfänge der Bemühungen um eine europäische wirtschaftliche und politische Integration eine gemeinsame Verkehrspolitik, die den Bau eines europäischen Wasserstrassennetzes einschloss, wahrscheinlicher als je zuvor.

Als Geograph beschäftigte sich der Verfasser auch mit dem Einfluss, den die Nutzung (oder auch Nicht-Nutzung) der Mosel auf die Völker und Wirtschaften der an die Mosel angrenzenden Räume ausübte. Jede Phase der Entwicklung wurde unter diesem Gesichtspunkt betrachtet. Der Verfasser schliesst mit einer Beurteilung des ersten Jahrzehnts der kanalisierten Mosel und versucht, einige Voraussagen über ihre künftige Rolle zu machen. In diesem Zusammenhang wurde eine zweite geographische Dimension erwähnt, nämlich, die wesentliche Funktion der Mosel als einer der drei wichtigen Binnenwasserwege zwischen dem Mittelmeer und der Nordsee (die beiden anderen sind die Mass und der Rhone-Rhein Kanal), mit allen Verflechtungen, die dieser Umstand für den Verkehr und andere Funktionen des Flusses bisher gehabt hat und noch haben könnte.

Schliesslich versucht der Verfasser zu zeigen, wie dieser grosse, natürliche Verkehrsweg bis vor kürzester Zeit wegen säkularer politischer Streite und Rivalität unterbenützt worden ist.

764739